100 20-MIN EASY RECIPES

100 20-MINUTE EASY RECIPES

Tempting ideas for healthy quick-cook meals, from light bites and energizing lunches to inspirational fish, meat and vegetable dishes

Contributing editor: Jenni Fleetwood

southwater

This edition is published by Southwater

Southwater is an imprint of Anness Publishing Ltd, Hermes House, 88–89 Blackfriars Road, London SE1 8HA tel. 020 7401 2077; fax 020 7633 9499; www.southwaterbooks.com; www.annesspublishing.com

If you like the images in this book and would like to investigate using them for publishing, promotions or advertising, please visit our website www.practicalpictures.com for more information.

Ethical Trading Policy

Because of our ongoing ecological investment programme, you, as our customer, can have the pleasure and reassurance of knowing that a tree is being cultivated on your behalf to naturally replace the materials used to make the book you are holding. For further information about this scheme, go to www.annesspublishing.com/trees

UK agent: The Manning Partnership Ltd, 6 The Old Dairy, Melcombe Road, Bath BA2 3LR;tel. 01225 478444; fax 01225 478440; sales@manning-partnership.co.uk

UK distributor: Grantham Book Services Ltd, Isaac Newton Way, Alma Park Industrial Estate, Grantham, Lincs NG31 9SD; tel. 01476 541080; fax 01476 541061; orders@gbs.tbs-ltd.co.uk

North American agent/distributor: National Book Network, 4501 Forbes Boulevard, Suite 200, Lanham, MD 20706; tel. 301 459 3366; fax 301 429 5746; www.nbnbooks.com

Australian agent/distributor: Pan Macmillan Australia, Level 18, St Martins Tower, 31 Market St, Sydney, NSW 2000; tel. 1300 135 113; fax 1300 135 103; customer.service@macmillan.com.au

New Zealand agent/distributor: David Bateman Ltd, 30 Tarndale Grove, Off Bush Road, Albany, Auckland; tel. (09) 415 7664; fax (09) 415 8892

Parts of this were previously published in a larger volume, *The 20-Minute Cookbook*.
A CIP catalogue record for this book is available from the British Library.

Publisher: Joanna Lorenz
Editorial Director: Helen Sudell
Project Editor: Catherine Stuart
Production Controller: Wendy Lawson
Book Design: Diane Pullen and Mike Morey
Cover Design: Balley Design
Contributors: Pepita Aris, Mridula Baljekar, Jane Bamforth, Alex Barker, Judy Bastyra, Georgina Campbell, Coralie Dorman, Matthew Drennan, Joanna Farrow, Maria Filippelli, Jenni Fleetwood, Christine France, Brian Glover, Juliet Harbutt, Simona Hill, Becky Johnson, Bridget Jones, Lucy Knox, Jane Milton, Suzannah Olivier, Keith Richmond, Rena Salaman, Marlena Spieler, Liz Trigg, Linda Tubby, Sunil Vijayakar, Jenny White, Biddy White-Lennon, Kate Whiteman, Rosemary Wilkinson, Jeni Wright
Photography: Karl Adamson, Edward Allwright, Caroline Barty, Steve Baxter, Martin Brigdale, Nicki Dowey, James Duncan, Michelle Garrett, John Heseltine, Amanda Heywood, Janine Hosegood, Don Last, William Lingwood, Craig Robertson and Sam Stowell

Main front cover image shows Kedgeree – for recipe, see page 22

3 5 7 9 10 8 6 4 2

Notes

Bracketed terms are intended for American readers.
For all recipes, quantities are given in both metric and imperial measures and, where appropriate, measures are also given in standard cups and spoons. Follow one set of measures, but not a mixture, because they are not interchangeable.
Standard spoon and cup measures are level.1 tsp = 5ml, 1 tbsp = 15ml, 1 cup = 250ml/8fl oz.
Australian standard tablespoons are 20ml. Australian readers should use 3 tsp in place of 1 tbsp for measuring small quantities of gelatine, flour, salt etc.
American pints are 16fl oz/2 cups. American readers should use 20fl oz/2.5 cups in place of 1 pint when measuring liquids.
Electric oven temperatures in this book are for conventional ovens. When using a fan oven, the temperature will probably need to be reduced by about 10–20°C/20–40°F. Since ovens vary, you should check with your manufacturer's instruction book for guidance.
The nutritional analysis given for each recipe is calculated per portion (i.e. serving or item), unless otherwise stated. If the recipe gives a range, such as Serves 4–6, then the nutritional analysis will be for the smaller portion size, i.e. 6 servings.
Measurements for sodium do not include salt added to taste.
Medium eggs (US large) are used unless otherwise stated.

CONTENTS

INTRODUCTION

As the pace of modern life accelerates, we often find ourselves juggling all kinds of priorities – relating to work, family and friends – and unwilling to take half-measures on any of them. When things are this busy, the matter of feeding ourselves and our loved ones seems virtually impossible without resorting to ready-prepared supermarket foods. Yet the convenience option is far from ideal in the long term, not only due to the obvious implications for a healthy balanced diet, but also because we are losing one of the greatest rewards of our daily routine: sharing and enjoying wholesome home-prepared food with those close to us.

The fact is, preparing a meal is not only a great way of spending quality time with family and friends, it is also a wonderful stress-reliever after a hectic day. But time remains an issue. You might have agreed to go out for after-work drinks, be rushing to get to an evening class, or simply have chores to do, work to finish, or be desperate to put your feet up for a couple of hours before going to bed. This is when you really need a selection of no-fuss recipes at your fingertips: lunches you can prepare and pack in next to no time; main course meals that raise your spirits without sapping your energy; and super-fast desserts that serve as a well-earned treat. This inspiring collection of dishes, all of which can be prepared and cooked in 20 minutes or less, are sure to satisfy the need for natural ingredients, fresh flavours and stress-free, mess-free kitchen time.

WHAT'S IN YOUR CUPBOARDS?

As any experienced cook will tell you, the secret of successful speedy cooking is to have all the essential quick-cook aids to hand. Take a look at the contents of your kitchen cupboards and drawers. You may have some delightful wine glasses and stunning serving dishes, but, in a practical sense, does the equipment meet your day-to-day needs?

Here are some of the things that are essential to every modern kitchen. You need a selection of good quality kitchen knives for cutting items both tough and tender, and a sound basis upon which to use them. Invest in a set of quality wooden and synthetic chopping boards, retaining specific boards for use with raw meat, cooked meat, fish and shellfish, and dairy products. Inspect your peelers and graters, too. These become blunted with age, so make sure your utensils still have their edge.

Next, weigh up your measuring equipment. A set of scales is handy, but for speed and convenience you should have at least one measuring jug

Above: Rolling pieces of chicken in a delicious, spicy coating before cooking can be done in minutes, and makes a delightful healthy treat for children.

(pitcher), plus a set of measuring cups to size up smaller quantities of liquids and dry goods during cooking.

Is it time to upgrade your pans and bakeware? Many meals require the use of at least two pans, but a minimum of three is essential for any kitchen. Large pans are best for boiling substantial quantities of food such as pasta and rice; medium-sized ones are superb for sauces and similar mixtures; and small pans are ideal for cooking solo, or for heating up small quantities of liquids.

Invest in a non-stick frying pan, and try to find one with an ovenproof handle and lid that can double as a shallow casserole dish. Similarly, every kitchen should have a griddle pan and wok. It's a mistake to associate these two with rather specific types of dish, as they can be put to use in all kinds of quick-cook recipes. And if you're stuck for inspiration, tossing tender morsels of meat, fish or vegetables with spices, and simply griddling or sautéeing over the heat, is hard to beat as flavoursome, no-fuss fare. Finally, baking sheets and roasting pans, usually associated with slower-to-cook dishes, are useful for holding ingredients and catching spills.

Left: However quick the dish, don't forget the presentation. A fresh, fragrant topping of rocket pesto, for example, makes a simple yet superb finishing touch.

Right: Sensational side dishes in this collection include the aromatic Masala Beans with Fenugreek. The spice mix for this dish is best prepared in a food processor or blender if possible – another handy quick-cook aid.

QUICK AND HEALTHY COOKING METHODS

Generally, when cooking over the hob, keep stirring spoons and spatulas to hand so that you can add and blend in ingredients as required. A free-standing metal colander will leave your hands free to empty heavy pans, while a sieve/strainer is useful for straining small quantities of cooked vegetables. Clean these items regularly with very hot, slightly soapy water to prevent them becoming clogged.

Items of bakeware can be put to task on savoury dishes as well as sweet. Escalopes can be flattened using a rolling pin before grilling or griddling, while a pastry brush is perfect for coating fish, meat or vegetables with marinade before or during cooking – a classic last-minute means of adding flavour. Skewers are not just for the barbecue: they can be used to sizzle smaller portions of meat when cooking under the grill – and are a healthy alternative to deep-frying.

Below: The bright colours and contrasting textures of Tofu and Pepper Kebabs are typical of the exciting vegetarian fare you'll find here.

ESSENTIAL INGREDIENTS

Another secret of no-fuss cooking is to adapt your favourite recipes to the foods you have to hand. Stock up on staples such as pasta and rice – buy healthier wholegrain if possible. Canned goods such as tomatoes and pulses are useful when there simply isn't the time for soaking or boiling. Don't forget the pesto, either. This versatile sauce is not only perfect for quick pasta, it is also a good 'mixer' for vegetable side dishes, such a mashed potatoes. Curry pastes and concentrated stocks will keep for several weeks in the refrigerator. There are some excellent shop-bought versions available, but, in the long run, making your own is more rewarding, and likely to be healthier. There are some useful recipes for stocks, as well as oils, marinades and dressings, in the pages that follow.

In terms of fresh foods, dairy items such as low-fat yogurt and crème fraîche are ideal for toning down heat and spice. And, of course, you should have a good stock of fresh fruits and vegetables on hand in the refrigerator. If you're ever stuck for what to buy, simply opt for a wide range of colours and textures. Useful flavour-boosters include fresh onions, garlic, chillies and handfuls of herbs – you may even get into the habit of growing your favourite herbs, to ensure you have a regular stock. Buy a lemon or lime or two as well: they're great for savoury marinades, or for serving on the side to squeeze over, and counteract, the richness of cooked fish or meat.

Remember that, in addition to forming the basis of some sumptuous main course meals, vegetables are the perfect complement to meat and fish dishes. While it's easy to remain in familiar territory by preparing traditional mashed potatoes or boiled green beans, an inspired twist or two can send the entire meal into another dimension. The very first chapter of this book introduces some superb tricks for creating simple but unique accompaniments.

Now you're equipped with all the essential culinary kit, read on for more tips on turning creative, quick cooking into an everyday event. There is just one note of caution to heed. The preparation and cooking times given with each of the following recipes should be treated as a guide only. We all have our own pace, and an experienced cook may take a little less time to prepare ingredients than a novice. But the wonderful thing about these recipes is that, whether you turn them around in ten minutes or twenty, their simplicity guarantees superb results every time.

20-MINUTE ESSENTIALS

Before you try your hand at some of the suggested recipes in this volume, give a little consideration to your condiments. It really helps to have a repertoire of stocks and flavoured oils to hand, all of which can be made in advance and will keep for some time under the right conditions. For a more instant flavour fix, there are also some quick and easy methods for making classic marinades and dressings — perfect partners for meat, fish or vegetables. If you do intend to make your own stocks and sauces, it's again worth assessing your equipment. Lighter blends can be easily whisked by hand, but thicker mixtures are best puréed using a hand-blender or the appropriate setting of a food processor. This section also contains some great ways of preparing vegetables and grains, some of which will do just as nicely as stand-alone snacks. Finally, there is a quick guide to the best breads on the market: ideal for mopping up soups or juices, or as a simple, wholesome complement to a main course dish.

Left: Fresh, home-prepared chicken stock is easy to make using left-over roast chicken, a few chunky vegetables and some suitable herbs and spices. Once prepared, it can be frozen, and will keep in the refrigerator for up to one month. A classic chicken stock recipe appears on the following pages.

BASICS: OILS, STOCKS, MARINADES AND DRESSINGS

Having a few ready-made basics, such as stocks, pasta sauces and flavoured oils, can really speed up everyday cooking. They can all be bought ready-made in the supermarket, but they are easy to make at home. Stocks take time to prepare, but they can be stored in the freezer for several months. Flavoured oils are straightforward and keep in the same way as ordinary oils so it's well worth having a few in the cupboard. All the basic sauces, dressings, marinades and flavoured creams on the following pages are simple to prepare and can either be made fresh or in advance.

FLAVOURED OILS

Good quality olive oil can be flavoured with herbs, spices and aromatics for drizzling, dressing and cooking.

Herb-infused oil

Half-fill a jar with washed and dried fresh herbs such as rosemary or basil. Pour over olive oil to cover, then seal the jar and place in a cool, dark place for 3 days. Strain the oil into a clean jar or bottle and discard the herbs.

Lemon oil

Finely pare the rind from one lemon, place on kitchen paper, and leave to dry for 1 day. Add the dried rind to a bottle of olive oil and leave to infuse for up to 3 days. Strain the oil into a clean bottle and discard the rind.

Chilli oil

Add several dried chillies to a bottle of olive oil and leave to infuse for about 2 weeks before using. If the flavour is

not sufficiently pronounced, leave for another week. The chillies can be left in the bottle and give a very decorative and colourful effect.

Garlic oil

Add several whole garlic cloves to a bottle of olive oil and leave to infuse for about 2 weeks before using. If the flavour is not sufficiently pronounced, leave the oil to infuse for another week, then strain the oil into a clean bottle and store in a cool, dark place.

STOCKS

When you have a little time on your hands, make stock. A supply of home-made stock in the freezer gives you the basis of dozens of quick and easy dishes, including risotto and a range of sauces. It's also a great way of using up leftover chicken, meat and fish, or a surplus of vegetables. To freeze, pour the cooled stock into 600ml/1 pint/ 2½ cup containers and freeze for up to 2 months.

Chicken stock

Put a 1.3kg/3lb chicken carcass into a large pan with 2 peeled and quartered onions, 2 halved carrots, 2 roughly chopped celery sticks, 1 bouquet garni, 1 peeled garlic clove and 5 black peppercorns. Pour in 1.2 litres/2 pints/ 5 cups cold water and bring to the boil. Reduce the heat, cover and simmer for 4–5 hours, regularly skimming off any scum from the surface and adding more water if needed. Strain the stock through a sieve (strainer) lined with kitchen paper and leave to cool.

Beef stock

Preheat the oven to 230°C/450°F/Gas 8. Put 1.8kg/4lb beef bones in a roasting pan and roast for 40 minutes, until browned, turning occasionally. Transfer the bones and vegetables to a large pan. Cover with water, add 2 chopped tomatoes and cook as for chicken stock.

Fish stock

Put 2 chopped onions, 1.3kg/3lb fish bones and heads, 300ml/½ pint/1¼ cups white wine, 5 black peppercorns and 1 bouquet garni in a large pan. Pour in 2 litres/3½ pints/9 cups water. Bring to the boil and simmer for 20 minutes, skimming often. Strain.

Vegetable stock

Put 900g/2lb chopped vegetables, including onions, leeks, tomatoes, carrots, parsnips and cabbage, in a large pan. Pour in 1.5 litres/2½ pints/ 6¼ cups water. Bring to the boil and simmer for 30 minutes, then strain.

MARINADES

These strong-tasting mixes are perfect for adding flavour to meat, poultry, fish and vegetables. Most ingredients should be marinated for at least 30 minutes.

Ginger and soy marinade

This is perfect for use with chicken and beef. Peel and grate a 2.5cm/1in piece of fresh root ginger and peel and finely chop a large garlic clove. In a small bowl, whisk 60ml/4 tbsp olive oil with 75ml/5 tbsp dark soy sauce. Season with ground black pepper and stir in the ginger and garlic.

Rosemary and garlic marinade

This is ideal for robust fish, lamb and chicken. Roughly chop the leaves from 3 fresh rosemary sprigs. Finely chop 2 garlic cloves and whisk with the rosemary, 75ml/5 tbsp olive oil and the juice of 1 lemon. Add the grated rind of the lemon too, if you like.

Lemon grass and lime marinade

Use this delicately-flavoured marinade with pieces of fish and chicken. Finely chop 1 lemon grass stalk. Whisk the grated rind and juice of 1 lime with 75ml/5 tbsp olive oil, salt and black pepper to taste, and the lemon grass.

Red wine and bay marinade

This easy-to-learn marinade is ideal for flavouring red meat, particularly if you want to soften the texture of tougher cuts. Whisk together 150ml/¼ pint/ ⅔ cup red wine, 1 finely chopped garlic clove, 2 torn fresh bay leaves and 45ml/3 tbsp olive oil. Season to taste with black pepper.

Below: Marinades containing red wine are particularly good for tenderizing tougher cuts of meat such as stewing steak.

DRESSINGS

Freshly made dressings are delicious drizzled over salads but are also tasty served with cooked vegetables and simply cooked fish, meat and poultry. You can make these dressings a few hours in advance and store them in a sealed container in the refrigerator until ready to use. Give them a quick whisk before drizzling over the food.

Honey and wholegrain mustard dressing

Drizzle this sweet, peppery dressing over leafy salads, fish, chicken and red meat dishes or toss with warm new potatoes. Whisk together 15ml/1 tbsp wholegrain mustard, 30ml/2 tbsp white wine vinegar, 15ml/1 tbsp honey and 75ml/5 tbsp extra virgin olive oil and season generously with salt and ground black pepper.

Orange and tarragon dressing

Serve this fresh, tangy dressing with salads and grilled (broiled) fish. In a small bowl, whisk the rind and juice of 1 large orange with 45ml/3 tbsp olive oil and 15ml/1 tbsp chopped fresh tarragon. Season with salt and plenty of ground black pepper to taste and chill before use if possible.

Toasted coriander and cumin dressing

Drizzle this warm, spicy dressing over grilled (broiled) chicken, lamb or beef. Heat a small frying pan and sprinkle in 15ml/1 tbsp each coriander and cumin seeds. Dry-fry until the seeds release their aromas and start to pop, then crush the seeds using a mortar and pestle. Add 45ml/3 tbsp olive oil, whisk to combine, then leave to infuse for 20 minutes. Season with salt and pepper to taste.

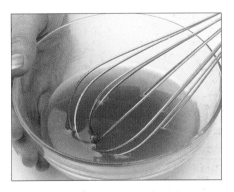

Lemon and horseradish dressing

This tangy dressing is particularly good with cooked beetroot. For a quick and easy lunch, serve it with smoked mackerel and a herb salad. There is no need to dress the salad – this delightfully creamy relish will do very nicely sitting on the side of the plate. In a small bowl, combine 30ml/2 tbsp freshly squeezed lemon juice and 30ml/2 tbsp mirin or dry sherry. Whisk well, then add 120ml/4fl oz/½ cup olive oil, continuing to whisk the dressing until it emulsifies. Whisk in 30ml/2 tbsp creamed horseradish. Taste the dressing, and add a little salt and black pepper, if you think it needs it. The dressing should be smooth in texture.

MAKING SIMPLE ACCOMPANIMENTS

When you've made a delicious main dish, you need to serve it with equally tasty accompaniments. The following section is full of simple, speedy ideas for fabulous side dishes – from creamy mashed potatoes, fragrant rice and spicy noodles to Italian-style polenta and simple, healthy vegetables.

MASHED POTATOES

Potatoes go well with just about any main dish. They can be cooked simply – boiled, steamed, fried or baked – but they are even better mashed with milk and butter.

Perfect mashed potatoes

Peel 675g/1½lb floury potatoes and cut them into large chunks. Place in a pan of salted boiling water. Return to the boil, then simmer for 15–20 minutes, or until completely tender. Drain the potatoes and return to the pan. Leave over a low heat for a couple of minutes, shaking the pan to drive off any excess moisture. Take the pan off the heat and, using a potato masher, mash the potatoes until smooth. Beat in 45–60ml/ 3–4 tbsp warm milk and a large knob (pat) of butter, then season with salt and pepper to taste.

Mustard mash

Make the mashed potatoes as directed above, then stir in 15–30ml/1–2 tbsp wholegrain mustard just before seasoning, and beat until smooth.

Parmesan and parsley mash

Make mashed potatoes as above, then stir in 30ml/2 tbsp freshly grated Parmesan and 15ml/1 tbsp chopped fresh flat leaf parsley.

Apple and thyme mash

Serve with pork. Make mashed potatoes as above. Heat 25g/1oz/2 tbsp butter in a pan and add 2 peeled, cored and sliced eating apples. Fry for 4–5 minutes, turning them often. Roughly mash, then fold into the potatoes, with 15ml/1 tbsp fresh thyme leaves.

Pesto mash

This is a simple way to dress up plain mashed potatoes. They have real bite and a lovely green-specked appearance. Make mashed potatoes as described above, then stir in 30ml/2 tbsp pesto sauce until thoroughly combined.

Masala mash

This tastes great with grilled (broiled) duck or pork. Put 15ml/1 tbsp mixed chopped fresh mint and coriander (cilantro) in a bowl. Add 5ml/1 tsp mango chutney, then stir in 5ml/1 tsp salt and 5ml/1 tsp crushed black peppercorns. Finely chop 1 fresh red and 1 fresh green chilli, removing the seeds if you like, and add to the mixture. Beat in 50g/2oz/¼ cup softened butter. Beat most of the herb mixture into the mashed potatoes and spoon the rest on top.

CRUSHED POTATOES

This chunky, modern version of mashed potatoes tastes fabulous. For all variations, simply crush the potatoes roughly, using the back of a fork.

Crushed potatoes with parsley and lemon

Cook 675g/1½lb new potatoes in salted boiling water for 15–20 minutes, until tender. Drain the potatoes and crush. Stir in 30ml/2 tbsp extra virgin olive oil, the grated rind and juice of 1 lemon and 30ml/2 tbsp chopped fresh flat leaf parsley. Season to taste.

Crushed potatoes with garlic and basil

Cook 675g/1½lb new potatoes in a pan of boiling salted water for 15–20 minutes until tender. Drain and crush. Stir in 30ml/2 tbsp extra virgin olive oil, 2 finely chopped garlic cloves and a handful of torn basil leaves. Season.

Crushed potatoes with pine nuts and Parmesan

Cook 675g/1½lb new potatoes in boiling salted water for 15–20 minutes until tender. Drain and crush. Stir in 30ml/ 2 tbsp extra virgin olive oil, 30ml/2 tbsp grated Parmesan cheese and 30ml/ 2 tbsp toasted pine nuts.

RICE

This versatile grain can be served simply – either boiled or steamed – or can be flavoured or stir-fried with different ingredients to make tasty, exciting accompaniments.

Easy egg-fried rice

Cook 115g/4oz/generous ½ cup long grain rice in a large pan of boiling water for 10–12 minutes, until tender. Drain well and refresh under cold running water. Spread out on a baking sheet and leave until completely cold. Heat 30ml/2 tbsp sunflower oil in a large frying pan and add 1 finely chopped garlic clove. Cook for 1 minute, then add the rice and stir-fry for 1 minute. Push the rice to the side of the pan and pour 1 beaten egg into the pan. Cook the egg until set, then break up with a fork and stir into the rice. Add a splash of soy sauce, and mix well.

Coconut rice

Put 225g/8oz/generous 1 cup basmati rice in a pan and pour in a 400ml/14oz can coconut milk. Cover with water, add some salt and bring to the boil. Simmer for 12 minutes, or until the rice is tender. Drain well and serve.

Coriander and spring onion rice

Cook 225g/8oz/generous 1 cup basmati rice in a large pan of salted boiling water for about 12 minutes, or until tender. Drain the rice well and return to the pan. Stir in 3 finely sliced spring onions (scallions) and a roughly chopped bunch of fresh coriander (cilantro) until well mixed, then serve.

NOODLES

There are many different types of noodles, all of which are quick to cook and make the perfect accompaniment to Chinese- and Asian-style stir-fries and curries. Serve them on their own, or toss them with a few simple flavourings. They can also be served cold as a simple salad.

Soy and sesame egg noodles

Cook a 250g/9oz packet of egg noodles according to the instructions on the packet. Drain well and tip the noodles into a large bowl. Drizzle over 30ml/2 tbsp dark soy sauce and 10ml/2 tsp sesame oil, then sprinkle over 15ml/1 tbsp toasted sesame seeds and toss well until thoroughly combined. These noodles will be delicious whether served hot, or cold as a salad.

Spicy peanut noodles

This simple and very tasty dish takes only minutes to make and is good on its own or with grilled (broiled) chicken. Cook a 250g/9oz packet of egg noodles according to the instructions on the packet, then drain. Heat 15ml/1 tbsp sunflower oil in a wok and add 30ml/2 tbsp crunchy peanut butter. Add a splash of cold water and a dash of soy sauce and stir the mixture over a gentle heat until thoroughly combined. Add the noodles to the pan and toss to coat in the peanut mixture. Sprinkle with fresh coriander (cilantro) to serve.

Chilli and spring onion noodles

Soak 115g/4oz flat rice noodles in cold water for 30 minutes, until softened. Tip into a colander and drain well. Heat 30ml/2 tbsp olive oil in a wok or large frying pan. Add 2 finely chopped garlic cloves and 1 seeded and finely chopped fresh red chilli and fry gently for 2 minutes. Slice a bunch of spring onions (scallions) and add to the pan. Cook for a minute or so, then stir in the rice noodles, combining them with the other ingredients until heated through. Season with salt and ground black pepper before serving.

POLENTA AND COUSCOUS

The cornerstones of Italian and north African cuisines respectively, polenta and couscous are useful alternatives to the usual potatoes, bread or pasta.

Polenta can be served in two ways – either soft, or set and cut into wedges and grilled (broiled) or fried. Soft polenta is rather like mashed potato, and can therefore be layered with other ingredients and baked, or simply used as a topping. Grilled or fried polenta has a much firmer texture and a lovely crisp shell. Traditional preparation of polenta requires lengthy boiling and constant attention during cooking, but the widely available quick-cook varieties give excellent results.

Similarly, the familiar commercial varieties of couscous involve quick and easy preparation. However, if you have a little time, the oven-baked preparation given here is hard to beat for its sublime flavour and perfect texture.

Soft polenta

Cook 225g/8oz/2 cups quick-cook polenta according to the instructions on the packet. As soon as the polenta is cooked, stir in about 50g/2oz/¼ cup butter. Season with salt and black pepper to taste, then serve immediately.

Soft polenta with Parmesan and sage

Cook 225g/8oz/2 cups quick-cook polenta according to the instructions on the packet. As soon as the polenta is cooked, stir in 115g/4oz/1⅓ cups freshly grated Parmesan cheese and a handful of chopped fresh sage. Stir in a large knob (pat) of butter and season with salt and ground black pepper to taste before serving.

Soft polenta with Cheddar cheese and thyme

Cook 225g/8oz/2 cups quick-cook polenta according to the instructions on the packet. As soon as the polenta is cooked, stir in 50g/2oz/½ cups grated Cheddar cheese and 30ml/2 tbsp chopped fresh thyme until thoroughly combined. Stir a large knob (pat) of butter into the cheesy polenta and season with salt and plenty of ground black pepper to taste before serving.

Fried chilli polenta triangles

Cook 225g/8oz/2 cups quick-cook polenta according to the instructions on the packet. Stir in 5ml/1 tsp dried chilli flakes, check the seasoning, adding more if necessary, and spread the mixture out on an oiled baking sheet to a thickness of about 1cm/½in. Leave the polenta until cold and completely set, then chill for about 20 minutes. Turn the polenta out on to a board and cut it into large squares, then cut each square into 2 triangles. Heat 30ml/ 2 tbsp olive oil in a large frying pan. Fry the triangles in the olive oil for 2–3 minutes on each side, until golden, then lift out and drain briefly on kitchen paper before serving.

Grilled polenta with Gorgonzola

Cook 225g/8oz/2 cups quick-cook polenta according to the instructions on the packet. Check the seasoning, adding more if necessary, and spread the mixture out on an oiled baking sheet to a thickness of about 1cm/½in. Leave the polenta until cold and completely set, then chill for about 20 minutes. Turn the polenta out on to a board and cut it into large squares, then cut each square into 2 triangles. Pre-heat the grill (broiler) and arrange the polenta triangles on the grill pan. Cook for about 5 minutes, or until golden brown, then turn over and top each triangle with a sliver of Gorgonzola. Grill (broil) for a further 5 minutes, or until bubbling.

Baked couscous

Stir 5ml/1 tsp salt into 600ml/1 pint/ 2½ cups warm water. Measure 500g/ 1¼lb/3 cups couscous into a bowl and add the salted water, stirring to make sure it is absorbed evenly. Leave to stand for 10 minutes to plump up, then, using your fingers, rub 45ml/3 tbsp sunflower oil into the grains, to air them and break up any lumps. Tip the couscous into an ovenproof dish, arrange about 25g/1oz/2 tbsp diced chilled butter over the top, and heat in the oven on 200°C/400°F/Gas 6 for about 20 minutes. Before serving, use your fingers again to work the melted butter into the grains to fluff them up, then pile the baked couscous onto a large serving dish and shape into a mound, ready to serve with the main part of the meal. If there are any leftover juices from the main dish, you can drizzle these over the top, if liked.

QUICK AND SIMPLE VEGETABLES

Fresh vegetables are an essential part of our diet. They are delicious cooked on their own but they can also be combined with other ingredients.

Stir-fried cabbage with nuts and smoky bacon

Heat 30ml/2 tbsp sunflower oil in a wok or large frying pan and add 4 roughly chopped rashers (strips) smoked streaky (fatty) bacon. Stir-fry for about 3 minutes, until the bacon starts to turn golden, then add ½ shredded green cabbage to the pan. Stir-fry for 3–4 minutes, until the cabbage is just tender. Season with salt and ground black pepper, and stir in 25g/1oz/¼ cup roughly chopped toasted hazelnuts or almonds just before serving.

Creamy stir-fried Brussels sprouts

Shred 450g/1lb Brussels sprouts and add to the pan. Heat 15ml/1 tbsp sunflower oil in a wok or large frying pan. Add 1 chopped garlic clove and stir-fry for about 30 seconds. Stir-fry for 3–4 minutes, until just tender. Season with salt and black pepper and stir in 30ml/2 tbsp crème fraîche. Warm through for 1 minute.

Honey-fried parsnips and celeriac

Peel 225g/8oz parsnips and 115g/4oz celeriac. Cut both into matchsticks. Heat 30ml/2 tbsp olive oil in a wok or large frying pan and add the parsnips and celeriac. Fry over a gentle heat for 6–7 minutes, stirring occasionally, until golden and tender. Season with salt and ground black pepper and stir in 15ml/1 tbsp clear honey. Allow to bubble for 1 minute before serving.

Glazed carrots

Clear honey is the magic ingredient to use with this carrot side dish too. Cut three large carrots into matchsticks. Steam them over a pan of boiling water for 2–4 minutes until just tender. Meanwhile, heat 25g/1oz/2 tbsp butter in a heavy pan, add 1 crushed garlic clove and 15ml/1 tbsp chopped fresh rosemary leaves and cook for 1 minute or until the garlic is golden brown. Add 5ml/1 tsp Dijon mustard and 10ml/2 tsp clear honey. Stir over the heat until the honey has melted into the buttery sauce, then add the carrots. Cook, tossing the carrots to coat them with the mixture, for 2 minutes until the carrots are glazed. Season lightly with salt, if needed, and serve immediately.

SPECIALIST BREADS

Bread makes a simple accompaniment to many meals and is the perfect ready-made side dish when time is short. Look out for part-baked breads that you can finish off in the oven, so you can enjoy all the benefits of freshly baked bread in just a few minutes.

Ciabatta This chewy Italian bread is long and oval in shape and is commonly available in ready-to-bake form. Look out for ciabatta with added sun-dried tomatoes or olives.

Focaccia This flat, dimpled Italian bread is made with olive oil and has a softer texture than ciabatta. It is available plain but is also often flavoured with fresh rosemary and garlic.

Naan Traditionally cooked in a clay oven, this Indian bread is easy to find in supermarkets and makes a tasty accompaniment to curries. It is available plain, and also flavoured with spices.

Chapati This Indian flatbread is less heavy than naan and makes a good alternative. The small, round breads can be a little more difficult to find but are worth searching for.

Soda bread This traditional Irish bread is made using buttermilk and bicarbonate of soda (baking soda). It has a delicious flavour and is great for mopping up sauces or serving with soups.

Above: Rosemary focaccia has a crumbly texture and is perfect for sandwiches and for serving with a whole range of Italian-style dishes.

LIGHT BITES AND LUNCHES

Light meals should lend themselves to speed, yet it's amazing how long we can spend deciding on the right thing to eat at the local coffee shop or supermarket, particularly when the range of sandwiches and snacks on offer is less than inspirational. The dishes in this chapter are, by contrast, bursting with colour and flavour – they use a range of classic deli ingredients, including cooked meats, salad, speciality breads and egg. Quick to prepare and just as easy to digest, they'll provide you with the vitality you need to see you through the rest of the day till you can finally sit down to a relaxing evening meal. The key thing here is having the right ingredients to hand – starting the week with a refrigerator full of fresh cheeses, smoked fish, fresh pasta, and so on will certainly help, but remember that leftovers from the weekend – cold roast chicken or ham, for example – can be put to great use in the week ahead. As well as chilled meals, there are also some great hot lunchtime treats: Steak and Blue Cheese on Ciabatta, Chicken Omelette Dippers or Warm Pasta Salad with Asparagus are all quick dishes with that extra special touch.

Left: Depending on the thickness of the meat, steaks can be griddled on both sides in a matter of minutes. To speed up the cooking time a little, you can try wrapping them in clear film and flattening with a rolling pin beforehand, but do make sure they are cooked right through before serving.

CHILLED TOMATO SOUP WITH ROCKET PESTO

THIS SOUP TAKES HARDLY ANY TIME TO MAKE, BUT MUST BE CHILLED, SO BEAR THAT IN MIND WHEN PLANNING YOUR MENU. WHIZZ IT UP WHEN YOU WAKE, AND MAKE THE PESTO JUST BEFORE SERVING.

Preparation: 10 minutes; Cooking: 4–5 minutes; Chilling: 4–8 hours

SERVES FOUR

INGREDIENTS
  225g/8oz cherry tomatoes, halved
  225g/8oz baby plum
    tomatoes, halved
  225g/8oz vine-ripened
    tomatoes, halved
  2 shallots, roughly chopped
  25ml/1½ tbsp sun-dried
    tomato purée (paste)
  600ml/1 pint/2½ cups
    vegetable stock
  salt and ground black pepper
  ice cubes, to serve
For the rocket pesto
  15g/½oz rocket (arugula) leaves
  75ml/5 tbsp olive oil
  15g/½oz/2 tbsp pine nuts
  1 garlic clove
  25g/1oz/⅓ cup freshly grated
    Parmesan cheese

1 Purée all the tomatoes and the shallots in a food processor or blender. Add the sun-dried tomato paste and process until smooth. Press the purée through a sieve (strainer) into a pan.

2 Add the vegetable stock and heat gently for 4–5 minutes. Season well. Pour into a bowl, leave to cool, then chill for at least 4 hours.

3 For the rocket pesto, put the rocket, oil, pine nuts and garlic in a food processor or blender and process to form a paste. Transfer to a bowl and stir in the Parmesan cheese. (This can also be prepared using a mortar and pestle.)

4 Ladle the soup into bowls and add a few ice cubes to each. Spoon some of the rocket pesto into the centre of each portion and serve.

Energy 218kcal/902kJ; Protein 4.8g; Carbohydrate 7.5g, of which sugars 7.2g; Fat 19g, of which saturates 3.6g; Cholesterol 6mg; Calcium 100mg; Fibre 2.2g; Sodium 104mg

GAZPACHO

PROBABLY THE MOST FAMOUS CHILLED SOUP IN THE WORLD, THIS ORIGINATED IN SPAIN BUT NOW APPEARS ON MENUS EVERYWHERE. IT IS PERFECT FOR A SUMMER LUNCH IN THE GARDEN.

Preparation: 12 minutes; Cooking: 5–6 minutes; Chilling: 4–8 hours

SERVES SIX

INGREDIENTS
  900g/2lb ripe tomatoes, peeled
    and seeded
  1 cucumber, peeled and
    roughly chopped
  2 red (bell) peppers, seeded and
    roughly chopped
  2 garlic cloves, crushed
  1 large onion, roughly chopped
  30ml/2 tbsp white wine vinegar
  120ml/4fl oz/½ cup olive oil
  250g/9oz/4½ cups fresh white
    breadcrumbs
  450ml/¾ pint/scant 2 cups iced water
  salt and ground black pepper
  ice cubes, to serve
For the garnish
  30–45ml/2–3 tbsp olive oil
  4 thick slices bread, crusts removed,
    cut into small cubes
  2 tomatoes, peeled, seeded and
    finely diced
  1 small green (bell) pepper, seeded
    and finely diced
  1 small onion, very finely sliced
  a small bunch of fresh flat leaf
    parsley, chopped

1 In a large bowl, mix the tomatoes, cucumber, peppers, garlic and onion. Stir in the vinegar, oil, breadcrumbs and water until well mixed. Purée the mixture in a food processor or blender until almost smooth, and pour into a large bowl. Stir in salt and pepper to taste and chill for at least 4 hours.

2 To make the garnish, heat the oil in a frying pan and add the bread cubes.

3 Fry over a medium heat for 5–6 minutes, stirring occasionally to brown evenly. Lift out the cubes with a slotted spoon, drain on kitchen paper and put into a small bowl. Place the remaining garnishing ingredients in separate bowls or on a serving plate.

COOK'S TIP
If the vegetable and vinegar mixture seems very thick after puréeing, stir in a little water. Cover the bowl with clear film before chilling the soup.

4 Ladle the gazpacho into bowls and add ice cubes to each portion. Serve at once. Pass around the bowls of garnishing ingredients with the soup.

Energy 412kcal/1730kJ; Protein 9.1g; Carbohydrate 55.6g, of which sugars 14.7g; Fat 18.6g, of which saturates 2.6g; Cholesterol 0mg; Calcium 109mg; Fibre 5g; Sodium 431mg

CHEESE TOASTIES

ALSO KNOWN AS BUBBLY CHEESE TOAST, BECAUSE OF THE WAY THE EGG AND CHEESE MIXTURE PUFFS UP DURING BAKING, THIS IS A NUTRITIOUS AND EASY SNACK THAT EVERYONE ENJOYS.

Preparation: 3–4 minutes; Cooking: 10–15 minutes

SERVES FOUR

INGREDIENTS

2 eggs
175–225g/6–8oz/1½–2 cups grated
  Cheddar cheese
5–10ml/1–2 tsp wholegrain mustard
4 slices bread, buttered
2–4 halved tomatoes (optional)
ground black pepper
watercress or fresh parsley,
  to serve (optional)

COOK'S TIP

For the best flavour, use a mature (sharp) Cheddar cheese or a mixture of Cheddar and Leicester. To save time, buy packets of ready-grated cheese from the supermarket.

1 Preheat the oven to 230°C/450°F/ Gas 8 (the top oven of a range-type stove is ideal for this recipe). Whisk the eggs lightly and stir in the grated cheese, mustard and pepper.

2 Lay the buttered bread face down in a shallow baking dish.

3 Divide the cheese mixture among the slices of bread, spreading it out evenly.

4 Bake in the oven for 10–15 minutes, or until well risen and golden brown, adding the halved tomatoes for a few minutes, if using. Serve immediately, with the tomatoes, and garnish with sprigs of watercress or parsley.

Energy 357kcal/1484kJ; Protein 16.6g; Carbohydrate 13.4g, of which sugars 0.8g; Fat 25.8g, of which saturates 15.5g; Cholesterol 159mg; Calcium 369mg; Fibre 0.4g; Sodium 552mg

FOCACCIA WITH SARDINES AND ROAST TOMATOES

FRESH SARDINES NOT ONLY HAVE A LOVELY FLAVOUR AND TEXTURE, BUT ARE ALSO CHEAP TO BUY
SO MAKE AN ECONOMICAL YET UTTERLY DELICIOUS LUNCH IN NEXT TO NO TIME.

Preparation: 3–4 minutes; Cooking: 15 minutes

SERVES FOUR

INGREDIENTS
   20 cherry tomatoes
   45ml/3 tbsp herb-infused olive oil
   12 fresh sardine fillets
   1 focaccia loaf
   salt and ground black pepper

VARIATIONS
This rather sumptuous topping tastes great on focaccia, but a split French stick would work just as well. If you happen to have some cold boiled potatoes in the refrigerator, slice them and fry them quickly in oil, while the sardines are cooking. Abandon the bread and pile the sardines and tomatoes on top of the potatoes instead.

1 Preheat the oven to 190°C/375°F/ Gas 5. Put the cherry tomatoes in a small roasting pan and drizzle 30ml/ 2 tbsp of the herb-infused olive oil over the top.

2 Season the tomatoes with salt and pepper and roast for 10–15 minutes, shaking the pan gently once or twice so that the tomatoes cook evenly on all sides. When they are tender and slightly charred, remove from the oven and set aside.

3 While the tomatoes are cooking, preheat the grill (broiler) to high. Brush the sardine fillets with the remaining oil and lay them on a baking sheet. Grill (broil) for 4–5 minutes on each side, until cooked through.

4 Split the focaccia in half horizontally and cut each piece in half to give four equal pieces. Toast the cut side under the grill. Top with the sardines and tomatoes and an extra drizzle of oil. Season with black pepper and serve.

Energy 301kcal/1262kJ; Protein 15.8g; Carbohydrate 27.6g, of which sugars 3.1g; Fat 15g, of which saturates 2.9g; Cholesterol 0mg; Calcium 106mg; Fibre 1.7g; Sodium 334mg

KEDGEREE

IMPRESS HOUSE GUESTS BY RUSTLING UP THIS DELECTABLE DISH IN LESS TIME THAN IT TAKES THEM TO TAKE A SHOWER. KEDGEREE IS GREAT FOR BREAKFAST, BRUNCH OR SUPPER.

Preparation: 2–3 minutes; Cooking: 16 minutes

SERVES FOUR

INGREDIENTS
  350g/12oz/1½ cups basmati rice
  225g/8oz undyed smoked
    haddock fillet
  4 eggs
  25g/1oz/2 tbsp butter
  30ml/2 tbsp garam masala
  ground black pepper

1 Preheat the grill (broiler) to medium. Place the smoked haddock on a baking sheet and grill (broil) for 10 minutes, or until cooked through.

2 Meanwhile, place the eggs in a pan of cold water and bring to the boil. Cook for 6–7 minutes. At the same time as the eggs and haddock are cooking, cook the rice in a pan of boiling water for 10–12 minutes.

3 When the eggs are cooked, drain and place under cold running water until cool enough to handle. Shell the eggs and cut into halves or quarters.

4 Remove the baking sheet from under the grill and transfer the smoked haddock to a board. Remove the skin when cool enough to handle.

5 Using a fork, ease the flesh apart so that it separates into large flakes. Remove any remaining bones.

6 Drain the rice and tip it into a bowl. Melt the butter in a pan, stir in the garam masala and add the fish. When it has warmed through, add it to the rice with the smoked fish and eggs. Mix gently, taking care not to mash the eggs. Season and serve immediately.

Energy 480kcal/2006kJ; Protein 23.5g; Carbohydrate 69.9g, of which sugars 0g; Fat 11.5g, of which saturates 4.9g; Cholesterol 224mg; Calcium 59mg; Fibre 0g; Sodium 536mg

HERRING FILLETS <u>IN</u> OATMEAL <u>WITH</u> APPLES

FRESH HERRINGS MAKE AN INEXPENSIVE AND TASTY SUPPER FISH. COATING THEM IN OATMEAL BEFORE FRYING GIVES THEM A CRISP OUTER EDGE THAT CONTRASTS WELL WITH THE TENDER APPLE SLICES.

Preparation: 3–4 minutes; Cooking: 6 minutes

SERVES FOUR

INGREDIENTS
8 herring fillets
seasoned flour, for coating
1 egg, beaten
115g/4oz/1 cup fine pinhead oatmeal
  or oatflakes
oil, for frying
2 eating apples
25g/1oz/2 tbsp butter

1 Wash the fish and pat dry with kitchen paper. Skin the fillets and check that all bones have been removed.

2 Toss the herring fillets in the seasoned flour, then dip them in the beaten egg and coat them evenly with the oatmeal or oatflakes.

3 Heat a little oil in a heavy frying pan and fry the fillets, a few at a time, until golden brown. Drain on kitchen paper and keep warm.

4 Core the apples, but do not peel. Slice them quite thinly. In another pan, melt the butter and fry the apple slices gently until just softened. Serve the apple with the coated fish fillets.

VARIATIONS
• Mackerel fillets can be cooked in the same way.
• A fruit sauce – apple, gooseberry or rhubarb – could be served instead of the sliced apples. Cook 225g/8oz of your preferred fruit with 90ml/6 tbsp cold water until just softened. Purée and serve with the fish.
• Try serving this with crisp grilled (broiled) bacon slices or follow the fruit theme by wrapping strips of bacon around pitted prunes that have been soaked in port, then grilling (broiling) the bacon rolls.
• Poached nectarine slices would also be a good accompaniment.

Energy 566kcal/2361kJ; Protein 35.6g; Carbohydrate 24.3g, of which sugars 3.4g; Fat 37g, of which saturates 9.9g; Cholesterol 146mg; Calcium 128mg; Fibre 2.6g; Sodium 270mg

CHOPPED EGGS AND ONIONS

QUICK AND EASY TO MAKE, THIS IS A SPEEDY LUNCH. YOU COULD EVEN PACK IT UP AND TAKE IT TO WORK, ALTHOUGH THE AROMA OF EGGS AND ONION MIGHT NOT PROVE IRRESISTIBLE TO EVERYONE.

Preparation: 3–4 minutes; Cooking: 12 minutes

SERVES FOUR TO SIX

INGREDIENTS
8–10 eggs
6–8 spring onions (scallions) and/or
   1 yellow or white onion, very finely
   chopped, plus extra to garnish
60–90ml/4–6 tbsp mayonnaise
mild French wholegrain mustard,
   to taste (optional)
15ml/1 tbsp chopped fresh parsley
salt and ground black pepper
rye toasts or crackers, to serve

COOK'S TIP
Holding a freshly boiled egg under cold running water helps to prevent the yolk from acquiring a greenish tinge where it meets the white.

1 Put the eggs in a large pan and pour in cold water to cover. Heat the water. When it boils, reduce the heat and simmer the eggs for 10 minutes. Stir the eggs twice so they cook evenly.

2 Drain the eggs, hold them under cold running water, then remove the shells, dry the eggs and chop roughly.

3 Place the chopped eggs in a large bowl. Add the onions, season with salt and pepper and mix well. Add enough mayonnaise to bind the mixture together. Stir in the mustard, if using, and the chopped parsley, or sprinkle the parsley on top to garnish. If you have time, chill the mixture before serving with rye toasts or crackers.

Energy 170kcal/706kJ; Protein 8.7g; Carbohydrate 0.5g, of which sugars 0.5g; Fat 15.1g, of which saturates 3.2g; Cholesterol 261mg; Calcium 48mg; Fibre 0.3g; Sodium 140mg

WARM PASTA SALAD WITH ASPARAGUS

TAGLIATELLE DRESSED WITH A CREAMY ASPARAGUS SAUCE IS THE BASIS FOR THIS SUSTAINING SALAD.
IF YOU'VE SPENT THE MORNING GARDENING OR PLAYING SPORT, THIS IS A GREAT QUICK LUNCH.

Preparation: 6 minutes; Cooking: 12 minutes

SERVES FOUR

INGREDIENTS
- 450g/1lb asparagus
- 450g/1lb dried tagliatelle
- 225g/8oz cooked ham, in 5mm/¼in-thick slices, cut into fingers
- 2 eggs, hard-boiled and sliced
- 50g/2oz Parmesan cheese
- salt and ground black pepper

For the dressing
- 50g/2oz cooked potato
- 75ml/5 tbsp olive oil
- 15ml/1 tbsp lemon juice
- 10ml/2 tsp Dijon mustard
- 120ml/4fl oz/½ cup vegetable stock

VARIATIONS
Use sliced chicken instead of the ham, or thin slices of softer Italian cheese, such as Fontina or Asiago.

1 Snap the asparagus spears and discard the tough woody ends. Cut the spears in half and cook the thicker halves in boiling salted water for 12 minutes, adding the tips after 6 minutes.

2 Meanwhile, boil the pasta in a large pan of salted water for 10–12 minutes until tender.

3 Drain the asparagus. Reserve the tips. Purée the remainder with the dressing ingredients until smooth.

4 Drain the pasta, toss with the asparagus sauce and cool slightly. Divide among four pasta plates. Top with the ham, hard-boiled eggs and asparagus tips. Shave Parmesan cheese over the top.

Energy 699kcal/2941kJ; Protein 35.4g; Carbohydrate 88.2g, of which sugars 6.6g; Fat 25.2g, of which saturates 6.3g; Cholesterol 140mg; Calcium 228mg; Fibre 5.3g; Sodium 852mg

WARM SALAD OF HAM AND NEW POTATOES

WITH A LIGHTLY SPICED NUTTY DRESSING, THIS WARM SALAD IS AS DELICIOUS AS IT IS FASHIONABLE,
AND AN EXCELLENT CHOICE FOR A CASUAL SUMMER SUPPER WITH FRIENDS.

Preparation: 3 minutes; Cooking: 15–17 minutes

SERVES FOUR

INGREDIENTS
    225g/8oz new potatoes, halved
     if large
    50g/2oz green beans
    115g/4oz young spinach leaves
    2 spring onions (scallions), sliced
    4 eggs, hard-boiled and quartered
    50g/2oz cooked ham, cut into strips
    juice of ½ lemon
    salt and ground black pepper
For the dressing
    60ml/4 tbsp olive oil
    5ml/1 tsp ground turmeric
    5ml/1 tsp ground cumin
    50g/2oz/⅓ cup shelled hazelnuts

1 Cook the potatoes in boiling salted water for 10–15 minutes, or until tender. Meanwhile, cook the beans in boiling salted water for 2 minutes.

2 Drain the potatoes and beans. Toss with the spinach and spring onions.

3 Arrange the hard-boiled egg quarters on the salad and sprinkle the strips of ham over the top. Drizzle with the lemon juice and season with plenty of salt and pepper.

4 Heat the dressing ingredients in a large frying pan and continue to cook, stirring frequently, until the nuts turn golden. Pour the hot, nutty dressing over the salad and serve immediately.

VARIATION
An even quicker salad can be made by using a 400g/14oz can of mixed beans and pulses instead of the potatoes. Drain and rinse the beans and pulses, then drain again.

Energy 318kcal/1319kJ; Protein 12.4g; Carbohydrate 11g, of which sugars 2.2g; Fat 25.4g, of which saturates 4g; Cholesterol 198mg; Calcium 106mg; Fibre 2.3g; Sodium 268mg

PASTA SALAD WITH SALAMI

THIS PASTA DISH IS EASY TO MAKE AND WOULD BE PERFECT FOR A PICNIC OR PACKED LUNCH.
TAKE THE DRESSING AND SALAD LEAVES SEPARATELY AND MIX EVERYTHING AT THE LAST MOMENT.

Preparation: 3–4 minutes; Cooking: 12 minutes

SERVES FOUR

INGREDIENTS
225g/8oz pasta twists
275g/10oz jar charcoal-roasted
  peppers in oil
115g/4oz/1 cup pitted black olives
4 drained sun-dried tomatoes
  in oil, quartered
115g/4oz Roquefort cheese,
  crumbled
10 slices peppered salami, cut
  into strips
115g/4oz packet mixed leaf salad
30ml/2 tbsp white wine vinegar
30ml/2 tbsp chopped fresh oregano
2 garlic cloves, crushed
salt and ground black pepper

1 Cook the pasta in a large pan of lightly salted boiling water for 12 minutes, or according to the instructions on the packet, until tender but not soft. Drain thoroughly and rinse with cold water, then drain again.

2 Drain the peppers and reserve 60ml/ 4 tbsp of the oil for the dressing. Cut the peppers into long, fine strips and mix them with the olives, sun-dried tomatoes and Roquefort in a large bowl. Stir in the pasta and peppered salami.

3 Divide the salad leaves among four individual bowls and spoon the pasta salad on top. Whisk the reserved oil with the vinegar, oregano, garlic and seasoning to taste. Spoon this dressing over the salad and serve at once.

VARIATION
Use chicken instead of the salami and cubes of Brie in place of the Roquefort.

Energy 429kcal/1797kJ; Protein 17.8g; Carbohydrate 46.7g, of which sugars 6.6g; Fat 20.3g, of which saturates 8.9g; Cholesterol 37mg; Calcium 188mg; Fibre 3.9g; Sodium 1341mg

ROAST CHICKEN PITTA POCKETS

FAMILIES OFTEN HAVE TO EAT IN RELAYS: A PARENT IS GOING TO BE HOME LATE; ONE CHILD HAS A MUSIC LESSON; ANOTHER IS OFF TO THE SKATE PARK. THIS SERVE-ANYTIME SNACK WILL SUIT THE LOT.

Preparation: 12–14 minutes; Cooking: 2 minutes

MAKES SIX

INGREDIENTS
1 small cucumber, peeled and diced
3 tomatoes, peeled, seeded
  and chopped
2 spring onions (scallions), chopped
30ml/2 tbsp olive oil
a small bunch of flat leaf parsley,
  finely chopped
a small bunch of mint,
  finely chopped
½ preserved lemon, finely chopped
45–60ml/3–4 tbsp tahini
juice of 1 lemon
2 garlic cloves, crushed
6 pitta breads
½ small roast chicken or
  2 large roast chicken breasts,
  cut into strips
salt and ground black pepper

1 Place the cucumber in a strainer over a bowl, sprinkle with a little salt and leave for 5 minutes to drain. Rinse well and drain again, then place in a bowl with the tomatoes and spring onions. Stir in the olive oil, parsley, mint and preserved lemon. Season well.

2 In a small bowl, mix the tahini with the lemon juice, then thin the mixture down with a little water to the consistency of thick double (heavy) cream. Beat in the garlic and season.

COOK'S TIP
The chicken in these pitta breads can be hot or cold – either roast a small bird specially or use up the leftovers from a large roast chicken.

3 Preheat the grill (broiler) to hot. Lightly toast the pitta breads well away from the heat source until they puff up. (Alternatively, lightly toast the breads in a toaster.) Open the breads and stuff them liberally with the chicken and salad. Drizzle a generous amount of tahini sauce into each one and serve with any extra salad.

Energy 337kcal/1419kJ; Protein 21g; Carbohydrate 43.5g, of which sugars 4.4g; Fat 9.9g, of which saturates 1.5g; Cholesterol 35mg; Calcium 182mg; Fibre 3.5g; Sodium 369mg

CHICKEN OMELETTE DIPPERS

HAVE YOU GOT A RELUCTANT EATER IN THE FAMILY? NOT ANY MORE. CHILDREN LOVE THESE PROTEIN-PACKED CHICKEN OMELETTE ROLLS. YOU MIGHT HAVE TO RATION THE KETCHUP, HOWEVER.

Preparation: 3 minutes; Cooking: 16 minutes

SERVES FOUR

INGREDIENTS

- 1 skinless, boneless chicken thigh, about 115g/4oz, cubed
- 40ml/8 tsp butter
- 1 small onion, chopped
- ½ carrot, diced
- 2 shiitake mushrooms, stems removed and chopped
- 15ml/1 tbsp finely chopped fresh parsley
- 225g/8oz/2 cups cooked long grain white rice
- 30ml/2 tbsp tomato ketchup, plus extra to serve
- 6 eggs, lightly beaten
- 60ml/4 tbsp milk
- 2.5ml/½ tsp salt, plus extra to season
- ground black pepper

1 Season the chicken. Melt 10ml/2 tsp butter in a frying pan. Fry the onion for 1 minute, then add the chicken and fry until cooked. Add the mushrooms and carrot, stir-fry over a medium heat until soft, then add the parsley. Set aside. Wipe the pan with kitchen paper.

2 Melt 10ml/2 tsp butter in the frying pan, add the rice and stir well. Mix in the fried ingredients, ketchup and black pepper. Stir well, adding salt to taste. Keep the mixture warm.

VARIATION

A mixture of tomato ketchup and chutney makes a tasty alternative dipping sauce.

3 Beat the eggs with the milk in a bowl. Stir in the measured salt, and add pepper. Melt 5ml/1 tsp of the remaining butter in an omelette pan. Pour in a quarter of the egg mixture and stir it briefly with a fork, then allow it to set for 1 minute. Using a fork, carefully place about a quarter of the rice mixture on top, slightly off-centre.

4 There are two ways of shaping the omelette. Either just flip it over the filling, then cut in half to make wedges, or roll the omelette around the filling and cut in half. Keep the filled omelette hot in a low oven while cooking three more. Serve two wedges or rolls per person, with a bowl of tomato ketchup on the side for dipping.

Energy 316kcal/1322kJ; Protein 18g; Carbohydrate 21.5g, of which sugars 3.7g; Fat 18.4g, of which saturates 8.1g; Cholesterol 338mg; Calcium 80mg; Fibre 0.5g; Sodium 322mg

MEXICAN TORTAS

THE GOOD THING ABOUT HOLLOWING OUT A BREAD ROLL IS THAT YOU CAN PACK IN MORE FILLING.
THIS MEXICAN SNACK USES ROAST PORK AND REFRIED BEANS BUT EXPERIMENTING IS EXPECTED.

Preparation: 5–6 minutes; Cooking: 0 minutes

SERVES FOUR

INGREDIENTS
    2 fresh jalapeño chillies
    juice of ½ lime
    2 French bread rolls or 2 pieces
      French bread
    75g/3oz/⅔ cup canned refried beans
    150g/5oz roast pork
    2 small tomatoes, sliced
    115g/4oz Cheddar or Monterey Jack
      cheese, sliced
    a small bunch of fresh coriander
      (cilantro)
    30ml/2 tbsp crème fraîche

1 Cut the chillies in half, scrape out the seeds, then cut the flesh into thin strips. Put it in a bowl, pour in the lime juice and leave to stand.

VARIATION
Sliced chicken carved from the rotisserie is another popular Mexican torta filler.

2 If using rolls, slice them in half and remove some of the crumb so that they are slightly hollowed. If using French bread, slice each piece in half lengthways.

3 Set the top of each piece of bread or roll aside and spread the bottom halves with a nice thick layer of the refried beans. Make sure the paste is evenly spread, as it will help to hold the next layer in place.

4 Cut the pork into thin shreds and put these on top of the refried beans. Top with the tomato slices. Drain the jalapeño strips and put them on top of the tomato slices. Add the cheese and sprinkle with coriander leaves.

5 Turn the top halves of the bread or rolls over so that the cut sides are uppermost, and spread these with crème fraîche. Sandwich back together again and serve.

Energy 307kcal/1285kJ; Protein 22.8g; Carbohydrate 18.2g, of which sugars 2.9g; Fat 15.8g, of which saturates 9.4g; Cholesterol 78mg; Calcium 271mg; Fibre 2g; Sodium 485mg

STEAK AND BLUE CHEESE ON CIABATTA

MANY PEOPLE PREFER THEIR STEAKS COOKED QUITE RARE IN THE CENTRE, BUT THEY ARE STILL DELICIOUS IF COOKED A LITTLE LONGER. ADD A COUPLE OF MINUTES TO THE COOKING TIME IF NECESSARY.

Preparation: 2–3 minutes; Cooking: 12–14 minutes

SERVES TWO

INGREDIENTS
1 part-baked ciabatta bread
2 ribeye steaks, about
  200g/7oz each
15ml/1 tbsp olive oil
115g/4oz Gorgonzola cheese, sliced
salt and ground black pepper

1 Bake the ciabatta according to the instructions on the packet. Remove from the oven and leave to rest while you cook the steak.

2 Heat a griddle pan until hot. Brush the steaks with the olive oil and lay them on the griddle pan. Cook for 2–3 minutes on each side, depending on the thickness of the steaks.

3 Remove the steaks and set them aside to rest. Meanwhile, cut the loaf in half and split each half horizontally.

4 Cut the steaks in half lengthways so each is only half as thick as before. Moisten the bread with the pan juices then make into sandwiches using the steak and cheese. Season well and serve.

COOK'S TIP
Part-baked bread cooks in about 8 minutes in a hot oven, but if even that is too long, just warm a regular baked ciabatta or French stick.

Energy 767kcal/3221kJ; Protein 66g; Carbohydrate 52g, of which sugars 3.1g; Fat 34.2g, of which saturates 15.8g; Cholesterol 161mg; Calcium 410mg; Fibre 2.3g; Sodium 1360mg

FISH AND SHELLFISH

There are few meats as well suited to quick cooking as fish and shellfish.
Filleted or whole, the best quality produce boasts soft, tender, flavoursome
flesh that is just as delicious grilled, griddled, barbecued or deep-fried. Fish
and shellfish also have a wonderful capacity to absorb flavour, even when
marinating is quick and done at the very last minute. The dishes here range
from sophisticated main course dishes such as Thai Steamed Mussels in
Coconut Milk, to classic comfort fare such as Fried Plaice with Tomato
Sauce and the unbeatable Fish and Chips. Some recipes take a minimal
approach to enhancing, and adding, flavour: grilling hake with a topping of
chilli flakes and grated lemon rind, for example, or steaming salmon fillets
solo. Others include a light, creamy sauce accompaniment based on fresh
fruits, vegetable-fruits or herbs. Whatever your choice, the versatility of fish
and shellfish mean that these recipes can be adapted to, and perfected for,
almost any occasion.

Left: Another great way to add flavour to fish is to smoke fillets, such as salmon, over aromatic coals.
This is very easy to do using a covered barbecue and a handful of soaked hickory wood chips.
The cooked fish is delicious hot or cold.

SEARED TUNA <u>WITH</u> SPICY WATERCRESS SALAD

TUNA STEAKS ARE WONDERFUL SEARED AND SERVED SLIGHTLY RARE WITH A PUNCHY SAUCE. IN THIS RECIPE A WATERCRESS SALAD IS SERVED JUST WARM AS A BED FOR THE TENDER FISH.

Preparation: 6 minutes; Cooking: 10 minutes

SERVES FOUR

INGREDIENTS
    30ml/2 tbsp olive oil
    5ml/1 tsp harissa
    5ml/1 tsp clear honey
    4 x 200g/7oz tuna steaks
    salt and ground black pepper
    lemon wedges, to serve
For the salad
    30ml/2 tbsp olive oil
    a little butter
    25g/1oz fresh root ginger, peeled
        and thinly sliced
    2 garlic cloves, finely sliced
    2 fresh green chillies, seeded and
        thinly sliced
    6 spring onions (scallions), cut into
        bitesize pieces
    2 large handfuls watercress
    1 lemon, cut into 4 wedges

1 Mix the olive oil, harissa, honey and salt, and rub it over the tuna steaks.

VARIATION
Prawns (shrimp) and scallops can be cooked in the same way. The shellfish will just need to be cooked through briefly – too long and they will become rubbery.

2 Heat a griddle or frying pan, grease it with a little oil and sear the tuna steaks for about 2 minutes on each side. They should still be pink on the inside.

3 Keep the tuna warm while you quickly prepare the salad: heat the olive oil and butter in a heavy pan. Stir in the ginger, garlic, chillies and spring onions, cook until the mixture begins to colour, then add the watercress. As soon as the watercress begins to wilt, toss in the lemon juice and season well with salt and plenty of ground black pepper.

4 Tip the warm salad on to a serving dish or individual plates. Slice the tuna steaks and arrange on top of the salad. Serve immediately with lemon wedges for squeezing over.

COOK'S TIP
Harissa is a North African spice paste based on chillies, garlic, coriander and cumin seeds. It is sold in tubes, like tomato purée (paste), or jars, or can be made fresh.

Energy 176kcal/731kJ; Protein 12.3g; Carbohydrate 1.6g, of which sugars 1.6g; Fat 13.4g, of which saturates 2.2g; Cholesterol 14mg; Calcium 18mg; Fibre 0.4g; Sodium 25mg

THAI STEAMED MUSSELS IN COCONUT MILK

AN IDEAL DISH FOR INFORMAL ENTERTAINING, MUSSELS STEAMED IN COCONUT MILK AND FRESH AROMATIC HERBS ARE QUICK AND EASY TO PREPARE AND GREAT FOR A RELAXED DINNER WITH FRIENDS.

Preparation: 10 minutes; Cooking: 6−7 minutes

SERVES FOUR

INGREDIENTS

1.6kg/3½lb mussels
15ml/1 tbsp sunflower oil
6 garlic cloves, roughly chopped
15ml/1 tbsp finely chopped fresh
  root ginger
2 large red chillies, seeded and
  finely sliced
6 spring onions (scallions),
  finely chopped
400ml/14fl oz/1⅔ cups coconut milk
45ml/3 tbsp light soy sauce
2 limes
5ml/1 tsp caster (superfine) sugar
a large handful of chopped
  coriander (cilantro)
salt and ground black pepper

1 Scrub the mussels in cold water. Scrape off any barnacles with a knife, then pull out and discard the fibrous "beard" visible between the hinge on any of the shells. Discard any mussels that are not tightly closed, or which fail to close when tapped sharply.

2 Heat a wok over a high heat and then add the oil. Stir in the garlic, ginger, chillies and spring onions and stir-fry for 30 seconds.

COOK'S TIP
The best-flavoured mussels are blue or European mussels from cold British waters. They are inexpensive, so don't be afraid to buy more than you need!

3 Grate the rind of the limes into the ginger mixture, then squeeze both fruit and add the juice to the wok with the coconut milk, soy sauce and sugar. Stir to mix.

4 Bring the mixture to the boil, then add the mussels. Return to the boil, cover and cook briskly for 5–6 minutes, or until all the mussels have opened. Discard any unopened mussels.

5 Remove the wok from the heat and stir in the chopped coriander. Season the mussels well with salt and pepper. Ladle into warmed bowls and serve immediately.

COOK'S TIP
For an informal supper with friends, take the wok straight to the table. There's something utterly irresistible about eating straight from the pan.

Energy 160kcal/679kJ; Protein 21.5g; Carbohydrate 6.7g, of which sugars 6.7g; Fat 5.5g, of which saturates 1g; Cholesterol 48mg; Calcium 272mg; Fibre 0.2g; Sodium 630mg

WARM SWORDFISH AND ROCKET SALAD

SWORDFISH IS ROBUST ENOUGH TO TAKE THE SHARP FLAVOURS OF ROCKET AND PECORINO CHEESE.
THE FISH CAN BE DRY, SO DON'T SKIP THE MARINATING STAGE UNLESS YOU'RE REALLY PUSHED.

Preparation: 7 minutes; Cooking: 8–12 minutes

SERVES FOUR

INGREDIENTS

4 swordfish steaks, about
   175g/6oz each
75ml/5 tbsp extra virgin olive oil,
   plus extra for serving
juice of 1 lemon
30ml/2 tbsp finely chopped
   fresh parsley
115g/4oz rocket (arugula) leaves,
   stalks removed
115g/4oz Pecorino cheese
salt and ground black pepper

1 Lay the swordfish steaks in a shallow dish. Mix 60ml/4 tbsp of the olive oil with the lemon juice. Pour over the fish. Season, sprinkle with parsley and turn the fish to coat. Cover the dish and leave to marinate for 5 minutes.

2 Heat a ridged griddle pan or the grill (broiler) until very hot. Take the fish out of the marinade and pat it dry with kitchen paper. Grill (broil) two steaks at a time for 2–3 minutes on each side until the swordfish is just cooked through, but still juicy.

3 Meanwhile, put the rocket leaves in a bowl and season with a little salt and plenty of pepper. Add the remaining 15ml/1 tbsp olive oil and toss well.

4 Place the swordfish steaks on four individual plates and arrange a little pile of salad on each steak. Shave the Pecorino over the top. Serve extra olive oil separately so it can be drizzled over the swordfish.

VARIATION
Tuna, shark or marlin steaks would be equally good in this recipe.

Energy 452kcal/1880kJ; Protein 43.6g; Carbohydrate 0.5g, of which sugars 0.4g; Fat 30.6g, of which saturates 9.5g; Cholesterol 101mg; Calcium 401mg; Fibre 0.6g; Sodium 581mg

GRIDDLED SWORDFISH WITH ROASTED TOMATOES

SLOW-ROASTING THE TOMATOES IS A GREAT TECHNIQUE WHEN YOU ARE ENTERTAINING AS THEY NEED NO LAST-MINUTE ATTENTION, BUT A MUCH QUICKER WAY IS SIMPLY TO GRILL THEM INSTEAD.
Preparation: 4 minutes; Cooking: 12 minutes, plus 3 hours if slow-roasting tomatoes

SERVES FOUR

INGREDIENTS
1kg/2¼lb large vine or plum
   tomatoes, peeled, halved
   and seeded
5–10ml/1–2 tsp ground cinnamon
a pinch of saffron threads
15ml/1 tbsp orange flower water
60ml/4 tbsp olive oil
45–60ml/3–4 tbsp sugar
4 x 225g/8oz swordfish steaks
rind of ½ preserved lemon,
   finely chopped
a small bunch of fresh coriander
   (cilantro), finely chopped
a handful of blanched almonds
a knob (pat) of butter
salt and ground black pepper

1 Preheat the oven to 110°C/225°F/ Gas ¼. Place the tomatoes on a baking sheet. Sprinkle with the cinnamon, saffron and orange flower water.

2 Trickle half the oil over, being sure to moisten every tomato half, and sprinkle with sugar. Place the tray in the bottom of the oven and cook the tomatoes for about 3 hours, then turn the oven off and leave them to cool. Alternatively, place under a medium grill (broiler) for 10 minutes.

VARIATION
If swordfish steaks are not available, use tuna or shark steaks.

3 Brush the remaining olive oil over the swordfish steaks and season with salt and pepper. Lightly oil a pre-heated cast-iron griddle and cook the steaks for 3–4 minutes on each side. Sprinkle the chopped preserved lemon and coriander over the steaks towards the end of the cooking time.

4 In a separate pan, fry the almonds in the butter until golden and sprinkle them over the tomatoes. Serve the steaks immediately with the tomatoes.

Energy 405kcal/1696kJ; Protein 42.3g; Carbohydrate 7.8g, of which sugars 7.8g; Fat 23g, of which saturates 5.2g; Cholesterol 98mg; Calcium 27mg; Fibre 2.5g; Sodium 330mg

CLASSIC FISH AND CHIPS

QUINTESSENTIALLY ENGLISH, THIS IS FISH AND CHIPS AS IT SHOULD BE COOKED, WITH TENDER FLAKES OF FISH IN A CRISP BATTER, AND DOUBLE-DIPPED CHIPS THAT ARE CHUNKIER THAN NORMAL FRIES.

Preparation: 5 minutes; Cooking: 14–15 minutes

SERVES FOUR

INGREDIENTS
  450g/1lb potatoes
  groundnut (peanut) oil,
    for deep-frying
  4 x 175g/6oz cod fillets, skinned
    and any tiny bones removed
For the batter
  75g/3oz/²⁄₃ cup plain
    (all-purpose) flour
  1 egg yolk
  10ml/2 tsp oil
  175ml/6fl oz/³⁄₄ cup water
  salt

1 To make the chips, cut the potatoes into 5mm/¼in thick slices. Then cut the slices into 5mm/¼in fingers or chips. Rinse the chips thoroughly in cold water, drain them well and then dry them thoroughly in a clean dish towel.

2 Heat the oil in a deep fat fryer to 180°C/350°F. Add the chips in the basket to the fryer and cook for 3 minutes. Lift out and shake off excess fat.

3 To make the batter, sift the flour into a bowl. Add a pinch of salt. Make a well in the middle of the flour and place the egg yolk in this. Add the oil and a little of the water. Mix the yolk with the oil and water, then add the remaining water and incorporate the surrounding flour to make a smooth batter. Cover and set aside until ready to use.

4 Reheat the oil in the fryer and cook the chips again for about 5 minutes, until they are golden and crisp. Drain on kitchen paper and season with salt. Keep hot in a low oven while you cook the pieces of fish.

COOK'S TIP
Use fresh rather than frozen fish for the very best texture and flavour. If you have to use frozen fish, thaw it thoroughly and make sure it is dry before coating with batter. Partially-frozen fish is unlikely to cook in the middle, despite the high cooking temperatures reached during deep-frying.

5 Dip the pieces of fish fillet into the batter and turn them to make sure they are evenly coated. Allow any excess batter to drip off before carefully lowering the fish into the hot oil.

6 Cook the fish for 5 minutes, turning once, if necessary, so that the batter browns evenly. The batter should be crisp and golden. Drain on kitchen paper. Serve at once, with lemon wedges and the chips.

VARIATIONS
• Although cod is the traditional choice for fish and chips, other white fish can be used: haddock is a popular alternative. Rock salmon, sometimes sold as huss or dogfish, also has a good flavour. Pollock or hoki are also suitable. Thin fillets, such as plaice or sole, tend to be too thin and can be overpowered by the batter. An egg and breadcrumb coating is more suitable for thin fish.
• To coat fish with egg and breadcrumbs, dip the fillets in seasoned flour, then in beaten egg and finally in fine, dry white breadcrumbs. Repeat a second time if the fish is to be deep-fried.
• Chunky chips are traditional with thick battered fish. Cut the potatoes into thick fingers to make chunky chips and allow slightly longer for the second frying.

Energy 645kcal/2700kJ; Protein 32.6g; Carbohydrate 54.3g, of which sugars 0.7g; Fat 34.5g, of which saturates 4.2g; Cholesterol 0mg; Calcium 130mg; Fibre 3.4g; Sodium 294mg

HADDOCK IN CIDER SAUCE

FIRST CLASS FISH DOESN'T NEED ELABORATE TREATMENT. THE CIDER SAUCE SERVED WITH THE HADDOCK IS BASED ON THE POACHING LIQUID, ENRICHED BY JUST A WHISPER OF CREAM.

Preparation: 2 minutes; Cooking: 13 minutes

SERVES FOUR

INGREDIENTS

675g/1½lb haddock fillet
1 medium onion, thinly sliced
1 bay leaf
2 parsley sprigs
10ml/2 tsp lemon juice
450ml/¾ pint/2 cups dry (hard) cider
25g/1oz/¼ cup cornflour (cornstarch)
30ml/2 tbsp single (light) cream
salt and ground black pepper

VARIATION
Try cod or hake or another white fish with firm flesh instead of haddock.

1 Cut the haddock fillet into four equal portions and place in a pan big enough to hold them neatly in a single layer. Add the onion, bay leaf, parsley and lemon. Season with salt.

2 Pour in most of the cider, reserving 30ml/2 tbsp for the sauce. Cover and bring to the boil, reduce the heat and simmer for 10 minutes, or until the fish is just cooked.

3 Strain 300ml/½ pint/1¼ cups of the cooking liquid into a measuring jug (cup). Cover the pan containing the fish and remove from the heat. In a small pan, mix the cornflour with the reserved cider, then gradually whisk in the measured cooking liquid and bring to the boil. Whisk until smooth and thick.

4 Whisk in more of the cooking liquid, if necessary, to make a pouring sauce. Remove the pan from the heat, stir in the cream and season to taste with salt and ground black pepper.

5 To serve, remove any skin from the fish, arrange on individual hot serving plates and pour the sauce over. Serve with a selection of vegetables.

Energy 216kcal/918kJ; Protein 32.5g; Carbohydrate 9.4g, of which sugars 3.5g; Fat 2.5g, of which saturates 1.1g; Cholesterol 65mg; Calcium 43mg; Fibre 0.1g; Sodium 127mg

STEAMED SALMON <u>WITH</u> CUCUMBER SAUCE

CUCUMBER AND FRESH DILL ARE A PERFECT COMBINATION IN THIS UNUSUAL HOT SAUCE, WHICH
COMPLEMENTS THE STEAMED SALMON. THE GARNISH MAKES THIS A PARTICULARLY PRETTY DISH.

Preparation: 5 minutes; Cooking: 15 minutes

SERVES FOUR

INGREDIENTS
 ½ lemon, thickly sliced
 3 fresh dill sprigs
 675g/1½lb piece thick salmon fillet
 orange slices and salad leaves,
  to serve
For the cucumber sauce:
 1 large cucumber, peeled
 25g/1oz/2 tbsp butter
 120ml/4fl oz/½ cup dry white wine
 45ml/3 tbsp finely chopped
  fresh dill
 60ml/4 tbsp sour cream
 salt and ground black pepper

1 To make the sauce, cut the cucumber in half lengthways, scoop out the seeds, then dice the flesh into a colander. Toss lightly with salt and leave to stand.

2 Half-fill a metal steamer with boiling water, fit the insert, making sure it is clear of the water, and spread out the lemon slices and herb sprigs on top. Lay the salmon over the herbs.

3 Make sure there is enough space on either side of the fish for air to circulate freely. Lay a sheet of baking parchment loosely over the fish, cover the steamer tightly with the lid or foil and place over a medium heat. Steam the salmon for about 15 minutes or until it flakes easily when tested with the tip of a knife blade.

4 About halfway through the steaming time, prepare the sauce. Rinse and dry the cucumber. Melt the butter in a frying pan and cook the cucumber for 2 minutes. Add the wine and boil until it evaporates. Stir in the dill and sour cream and season lightly. Cut the fish into portions. Serve with the sauce, orange slices and salad leaves.

Energy 406kcal/1686kJ; Protein 35g; Carbohydrate 1.5g, of which sugars 1.5g; Fat 26.7g, of which saturates 8.3g; Cholesterol 107mg; Calcium 62mg; Fibre 0.3g; Sodium 123mg.

HOT SMOKED SALMON

THIS IS A FANTASTIC WAY OF SMOKING SALMON ON A BARBECUE IN NO TIME AT ALL. THE MOJO MAKES A MILDLY SPICY COMPANION.

Preparation: 5 minutes; Cooking: 11–13 minutes, plus soaking

SERVES 6

INGREDIENTS
6 salmon fillets, each about 175g/6oz, with skin
15ml/1 tbsp sunflower oil
salt and ground black pepper
2 handfuls hickory wood chips, soaked in cold water for as much time as you have available, preferably 30 minutes
For the mojo
1 ripe mango, diced
4 drained canned pineapple slices, diced
1 small red onion, finely chopped
1 fresh long mild red chilli, seeded and finely chopped
15ml/1 tbsp good quality sweet chilli sauce
grated rind and juice of 1 lime
leaves from 1 small lemon basil plant or 45ml/3 tbsp fresh coriander (cilantro) leaves, shredded or chopped

1 First, make the mojo by putting the mango, diced pineapple, chopped onion, and seeded and chopped chilli together in a bowl.

2 Add the chilli sauce, lime rind and juice, and the herb leaves. Stir to mix well. Cover tightly and leave in a cool place until needed.

3 Rinse the salmon fillets and pat dry, then brush each with a little oil.

4 Place the fillets skin side down on a lightly oiled grill rack over medium-hot coals. Cover the barbecue with a lid or tented heavy-duty foil and cook the fish for 3–5 minutes.

5 Drain the hickory chips into a colander and sprinkle about a third of them as evenly as possible over the coals. Carefully drop them through the slats in the grill racks, taking care not to scatter the ash as you do so.

6 Replace the barbecue cover and continue cooking for a further 8 minutes, adding a small handful of hickory chips twice more during this time. Serve the salmon hot or cold, with the mojo.

COOK'S TIP
When sweet pineapples are in season, you may prefer to use fresh ones in the mojo. You will need about half a medium pineapple. Slice off the skin, remove the core and cut the flesh into chunks.

Energy 364kcal/1519kJ; Protein 35.9g; Carbohydrate 7.8g, of which sugars 7.4g; Fat 21.2g, of which saturates 3.6g; Cholesterol 88mg; Calcium 58mg; Fibre 1.3g; Sodium 82mg

FRIED PLAICE ^{WITH} TOMATO SAUCE

THIS SIMPLE DISH IS PERENNIALLY POPULAR WITH CHILDREN. IT WORKS EQUALLY WELL WITH LEMON SOLE OR DABS, WHICH DO NOT NEED SKINNING, OR FILLETS OF HADDOCK AND WHITING.

Preparation: 5 minutes; Cooking: 14 minutes

SERVES FOUR

INGREDIENTS

    25g/1oz/¼ cup plain (all-purpose) flour
    2 eggs, beaten
    75g/3oz/¾ cup dried breadcrumbs,
      preferably home-made
    4 small plaice or flounder, skinned
    25g/1oz/2 tbsp butter
    30ml/2 tbsp sunflower oil
    salt and ground black pepper
    fresh basil leaves, to garnish
    1 lemon, quartered, to serve
For the tomato sauce
    30ml/2 tbsp olive oil
    1 red onion, finely chopped
    1 garlic clove, finely chopped
    400g/14oz can chopped tomatoes
    15ml/1 tbsp tomato purée (paste)
    15ml/1 tbsp torn fresh basil leaves

1 First make the tomato sauce. Heat the olive oil in a large pan, add the finely chopped onion and garlic and cook for about 2–3 minutes, until softened.

2 Stir in the chopped tomatoes and tomato purée and simmer for 10 minutes, or until the fish is ready to be served, stirring occasionally.

3 Meanwhile, spread out the flour in a shallow dish, pour the beaten eggs into another and spread out the breadcrumbs in a third.

4 Season the fish with salt and pepper. Hold a fish in your left hand and dip it first in flour, then in egg and finally in the breadcrumbs, patting the crumbs on with your dry right hand. Aim for an even coating that is not too thick. Shake off any excess crumbs and set aside while you prepare the frying pans.

5 Heat the butter and oil in two large frying pans until foaming. Fry the fish for about 5 minutes on each side, until golden brown and cooked through. Drain on kitchen paper. Season the tomato sauce, stir in the basil and serve with the fish, garnished with basil leaves. Offer lemon wedges separately.

Energy 417kcal/1738kJ; Protein 28.1g; Carbohydrate 17.7g, of which sugars 4.9g; Fat 26.4g, of which saturates 3.1g; Cholesterol 0mg; Calcium 113mg; Fibre 1.6g; Sodium 349mg

GRILLED HAKE WITH LEMON AND CHILLI

NOTHING COULD BE SIMPLER THAN PERFECTLY GRILLED FISH WITH A DUSTING OF CHILLI AND LEMON RIND. THIS IS AN IDEAL MEAL FOR THOSE OCCASIONS WHEN SOMETHING LIGHT IS CALLED FOR.

Preparation: 2 minutes; Cooking: 6–8 minutes

SERVES FOUR

INGREDIENTS

    4 hake fillets, each 150g/5oz
    30ml/2 tbsp olive oil
    finely grated rind and juice of
      1 lemon
    15ml/1 tbsp crushed chilli flakes
    salt and ground black pepper

VARIATION

Any firm white fish can be cooked in this simple, low-fat way. Try cod, halibut or hoki. If you haven't got any chilli flakes, brush the fish with chilli oil instead of olive oil.

1 Preheat the grill (broiler) to high. Brush the hake fillets all over with the olive oil and place them skin side up on a baking sheet.

2 Grill (broil) the fish for 4–5 minutes, until the skin is crispy, then carefully turn the fillets over in the pan, using a metal spatula.

3 Sprinkle the fillets with the lemon rind and chilli flakes and season with salt and ground black pepper.

4 Grill the fillets for a further 2–3 minutes, or until the hake is cooked through. (Test using the point of a sharp knife; the flesh should flake.) Squeeze over the lemon juice just before serving.

Energy 188kcal/786kJ; Protein 27g; Carbohydrate 0.1g, of which sugars 0.1g; Fat 8.8g, of which saturates 1.2g; Cholesterol 35mg; Calcium 22mg; Fibre 0g; Sodium 150mg

POULTRY

Many of us have tried cobbling together a quick chicken stir-fry when time is tight, and experienced disappointment in the rather bland results. Stir-in sauces are often praised by advertisers for their speed, but they simply cannot compete with the aromatic contribution of fresh Thai basil, coriander or mint. In addition to some terrifically tasty home-made stir-fry dishes, this chapter draws on Mediterranean cooking styles to produce superlative pan-fried dishes, flavoured with fennel seeds or pesto. Like some fish, chicken is delightful coated in crumbs, and crumbed breast fillets served with spicy mayonnaise or stuffed with ham and cheese are a sure-fire wholesome favourite for children. Nor are other meats such as turkey and duck overlooked — the dishes included here are a savoury delight, ranging from the luxurious Turkey with Masala Cream Sauce to the Chinese-inspired Gingered Duck with Tamari and Mirin — griddled, sliced and rolled in warm, floury pancakes, all in less than 20 minutes!

Left: Crème fraîche and Coriander Chicken is a heavenly marriage of simplicity, freshness and fragrance. Prepared and cooked in minutes, it is a sure-to-impress standby dish for when friends call unexpectedly.

SOY SAUCE AND STAR ANISE CHICKEN

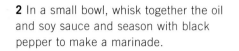

ALTHOUGH THE CHICKEN COOKS QUICKLY, IT DOES BENEFIT FROM BEING MARINATED FIRST. THIS ONLY TAKES A MOMENT AND THERE'LL BE NO LAST-MINUTE WORK TO DO WHEN GUESTS ARRIVE.

Preparation: 3–4 minutes; Cooking: 16 minutes, plus marinating time (optional)

SERVES FOUR

INGREDIENTS
4 skinless chicken breast fillets
2 whole star anise
45ml/3 tbsp olive oil
30ml/2 tbsp soy sauce
ground black pepper

1 Put the chicken breast fillets in a shallow, non-metallic dish and add the star anise.

2 In a small bowl, whisk together the oil and soy sauce and season with black pepper to make a marinade.

3 Pour the marinade over the chicken and stir to coat each breast fillet all over. Cover the dish with clear film (plastic wrap) and set aside for as much time as you have. If you are able to make it ahead, leave the chicken in the marinade for around 6–8 hours as the flavour will be improved. Place the covered dish in the refrigerator.

4 Cook the chicken under the grill (broiler), turning occasionally. It will need about 8 minutes on each side. Serve immediately.

VARIATION
If you prefer, cook on a barbecue. When the coals are dusted with ash, spread them out evenly. Remove the chicken breasts from the marinade and cook for 8 minutes on each side, spooning over the marinade from time to time, until the chicken is cooked through.

Energy 237kcal/992kJ; Protein 36.2g; Carbohydrate 0.6g, of which sugars 0.6g; Fat 9.9g, of which saturates 1.6g; Cholesterol 105mg; Calcium 9mg; Fibre 0g; Sodium 624mg

CRISPY FIVE-SPICE CHICKEN

STRIPS OF CHICKEN FILLET, WITH A SPICED RICE FLOUR COATING, BECOME DELICIOUSLY CRISP AND GOLDEN WHEN FRIED. THEY MAKE A GREAT MEAL WHEN SERVED ON STIR-FRIED VEGETABLE NOODLES.

Preparation: 5 minutes; Cooking: 10–12 minutes

SERVES FOUR

INGREDIENTS

200g/7oz thin egg noodles
30ml/2 tbsp sunflower oil
2 garlic cloves, very thinly sliced
1 fresh red chilli, seeded and sliced
½ red (bell) pepper, very
  thinly sliced
2 carrots, peeled and cut into
  thin strips
300g/11oz Chinese broccoli or
  Chinese greens, roughly sliced
45ml/3 tbsp hoisin sauce
45ml/3 tbsp soy sauce
5ml/1 tsp caster (superfine) sugar
4 skinless chicken breast fillets,
  cut into strips
2 egg whites, lightly beaten
115g/4oz/1 cup rice flour
15ml/1 tbsp five-spice powder
salt and ground black pepper
vegetable oil, for frying

1 Cook the noodles according to the packet instructions, drain and set aside.

2 Heat the sunflower oil in a wok, then add the garlic, chilli, red pepper, carrots and broccoli or greens and stir-fry over a high heat for 2–3 minutes.

3 Add the sauces and sugar to the wok and cook for a further 2–3 minutes. Add the drained noodles, toss to combine, then remove from the heat, cover and keep warm.

4 Dip the chicken strips into the egg white. Combine the rice flour and five-spice powder in a shallow dish and season. Add the chicken strips to the flour mixture and toss to coat.

5 Heat about 2.5cm/1½in oil in a clean wok. When hot, shallow-fry the chicken for 3–4 minutes until crisp and golden.

6 To serve, divide the noodle mixture between warmed plates or bowls and top each serving with the chicken.

VARIATION
Instead of the vegetables listed above for the stir-fry, try a mixture of mangetouts (snow peas), baby corn, orange (bell) peppers, spring onions (scallions) and celery.

Energy 574kcal/2419kJ; Protein 49.6g; Carbohydrate 68g, of which sugars 9.4g; Fat 12.3g, of which saturates 2.5g; Cholesterol 120mg; Calcium 83mg; Fibre 5.1g; Sodium 1210mg

SPICED CHICKEN RISOTTO WITH MINT

A CLASSIC RISOTTO MUST BE STIRRED FOR AROUND 20 MINUTES, WHICH CAN BE A LABOUR OF LOVE, BUT WHEN ROMANCE IS THE LAST THING ON YOUR MIND, THIS QUICK VERSION IS A GOOD ALTERNATIVE.

Preparation: 3–5 minutes; Cooking: 15–17 minutes

SERVES FOUR

INGREDIENTS
250g/9oz skinless, boneless chicken
  breast portions, diced
3 garlic cloves, chopped
5ml/1 tsp ground turmeric
30–45ml/2–3 tbsp olive oil
2 medium carrots, diced
seeds from 6–8 cardamom pods
500g/1¼lb/2½ cups long grain rice
250g/9oz tomatoes, chopped
750ml/1¼ pints/3 cups
  chicken stock
For the lemon and mint relish
3 tomatoes, diced
1 bunch or large handful fresh
  mint, chopped
5–8 spring onions (scallions),
  thinly sliced
juice of 2 lemons
salt

1 Mix the diced chicken with half the garlic and the turmeric. Heat a little of the oil in a pan, add the chicken and fry until the chicken has cooked through thoroughly. Remove from the pan and set aside.

2 Add the remaining oil, garlic and cardamom seeds with the carrots and rice. Stir-fry for 1–2 minutes.

3 Add the tomatoes and chicken stock to the pan and bring to the boil. Cover and simmer for about 10 minutes.

4 Meanwhile, make the relish by mixing all the ingredients in a bowl.

5 When the rice is almost cooked, fork in the chicken and heat through. Serve with the relish.

VARIATIONS
• Use the same quantity of pumpkin or butternut squash in place of the carrots.
• To make a vegetarian version, omit the chicken and add a drained 400g/14oz can of chickpeas to the rice just before the end of cooking.

Energy 600kcal/2511kJ; Protein 26g; Carbohydrate 105.9g, of which sugars 5.3g; Fat 7.4g, of which saturates 1.1g; Cholesterol 44mg; Calcium 73mg; Fibre 1.8g; Sodium 55mg

CHICKEN FRIED RICE

THIS STIR-FRY IS BASED ON COOKED RICE, SO IS IDEAL FOR USING UP YESTERDAY'S LEFTOVERS. ANY RICE WILL DO, BUT JASMINE HAS THE BEST FLAVOUR, ESPECIALLY IF COOKED IN COCONUT MILK.

Preparation: 4–5 minutes; Cooking: 10–12 minutes

SERVES FOUR

INGREDIENTS
30ml/2 tbsp groundnut (peanut) oil
1 small onion, finely chopped
2 garlic cloves, chopped
2.5cm/1in piece fresh root ginger,
   peeled and grated
225g/8oz skinless, boneless chicken
   breast portions, cut into
   1cm/½in dice
450g/1lb/4 cups cold cooked white
   long grain rice
1 red (bell) pepper, seeded and sliced
115g/4oz/1 cup drained canned
   whole kernel corn
5ml/1 tsp chilli oil
5ml/1 tsp hot curry powder
2 eggs, beaten
salt
spring onion (scallion) shreds,
   to garnish

2 Push the onion mixture to the sides of the wok, add the chicken to the centre and stir-fry for 2 minutes. Add the rice and toss well. Stir-fry over a high heat for about 3 minutes more, until the chicken is cooked through.

3 Stir in the sliced red pepper, corn, chilli oil and curry powder, with salt to taste. Toss over the heat for 1 minute. Stir in the beaten eggs and cook for 1 minute more. Garnish with the spring onion shreds and serve.

1 Heat the oil in a wok. Add the onion and stir-fry over a medium heat for 1 minute, then add the garlic and ginger and stir-fry for 2 minutes more.

COOK'S TIP
If you don't have any cold cooked rice in the refrigerator, you can still make this stir-fry if you have a couple of pouches of instant or express long grain or basmati rice in the cupboard. This type of rice cooks in under 2 minutes. For a stir-fry, the rice should be cold, so spread it out on a baking sheet after cooking and fan it to cool it quickly.

Energy 356kcal/1500kJ; Protein 21g; Carbohydrate 46.4g, of which sugars 6.3g; Fat 10.9g, of which saturates 2.5g; Cholesterol 135mg; Calcium 46mg; Fibre 1.4g; Sodium 150mg

STIR-FRIED CHICKEN WITH THAI BASIL

ON THE TABLE IN UNDER 10 MINUTES – YOU CAN'T SAY BETTER THAN THAT. THIS THAI-INSPIRED STIR-FRY IS TASTY, COLOURFUL AND FULL OF FLAVOUR, PERFECT FOR ANY DAY OF THE WEEK.

Preparation: 2–3 minutes; Cooking: 5–7 minutes

SERVES FOUR

INGREDIENTS
  4 skinless chicken breast fillets
  2 red (bell) peppers
  30ml/2 tbsp garlic-infused olive oil
  1 small bunch fresh Thai basil
  salt and ground black pepper

COOK'S TIP
Thai basil, sometimes called holy basil, has purple-tinged leaves and a more pronounced, slightly aniseedy flavour than the usual varieties. It is available in most Asian food stores but if you can't find any, use a handful of ordinary basil instead. Serve this fragrant stir-fry with plain steamed rice or boiled noodles and soy sauce on the side.

1 Using a sharp knife, slice the chicken breast portions into strips. Halve the peppers, remove the seeds, then cut each piece of pepper into strips.

2 Heat a wok or large frying pan. Add the oil. When it is hot, add the chicken and toss over the heat for 2 minutes.

3 Add the red peppers and continue to stir-fry the mixture over a high heat for about 3 minutes, until the chicken is golden and cooked through. Season with salt and ground black pepper.

4 Roughly tear up the basil leaves, add to the chicken and peppers and toss briefly to combine. Serve immediately.

Energy 211kcal/892kJ; Protein 37.8g; Carbohydrate 6.9g, of which sugars 5.4g; Fat 3.7g, of which saturates 0.8g; Cholesterol 105mg; Calcium 67mg; Fibre 1.4g; Sodium 97mg

CRÈME FRAÎCHE AND CORIANDER CHICKEN

THIS IS AN ANY-OCCASION MAIN COURSE DISH THAT CAN BE TURNED AROUND IN MINUTES. BE GENEROUS WITH THE CORIANDER LEAVES, AS THEY HAVE A WONDERFUL FRAGRANT FLAVOUR.

Preparation: 8 minutes; Cooking: 8 minutes

SERVES FOUR

INGREDIENTS
  6 skinless, boneless chicken
    thigh portions
  60ml/4 tbsp crème fraîche
  1 small bunch fresh coriander
    (cilantro), roughly chopped
  15ml/1 tbsp sunflower oil
  salt and ground black pepper

COOK'S TIP
This recipe uses boneless chicken thighs, but boneless breast portions can be used instead. Simply cut into bitesize pieces and cook in the frying pan for 5–6 minutes, until just tender.

1 Using a sharp cook's knife or cleaver, cut each chicken thigh into three or four pieces.

2 Heat the oil in a large frying pan, add the chicken and cook for about 6 minutes, turning occasionally.

3 Add the crème fraîche to the pan and stir until melted, then allow the mixture to bubble for 1–2 minutes. Add the chopped coriander to the chicken and stir to combine. Season with salt and ground black pepper to taste, and serve immediately.

Energy 249kcal/1041kJ; Protein 32.1g; Carbohydrate 0.7g, of which sugars 0.6g; Fat 13.1g, of which saturates 5.6g; Cholesterol 174mg; Calcium 44mg; Fibre 0.6g; Sodium 143mg

GREEK-STYLE CHICKEN WITH FENNEL SEEDS

THE SAUCE FOR THE CHICKEN IS BASED ON AVGOLEMONO, AN EXQUISITE EGG AND LEMON MIXTURE WHICH IS ONE OF GREECE'S GIFTS TO GOOD COOKS EVERYWHERE. IT TASTES GREAT WITH THE FENNEL.

Preparation: 3–4 minutes; Cooking: 15 minutes

SERVES FOUR

INGREDIENTS

4 skinless, boneless chicken
  breast portions
plain (all-purpose) flour, for dusting
30–45ml/2–3 tbsp olive oil
1–2 onions, chopped
¼ fennel bulb, chopped (optional)
15ml/1 tbsp chopped fresh parsley,
  plus extra to garnish
7.5ml/1½ tsp fennel seeds
75ml/5 tbsp dry Marsala
120ml/4fl oz/½ cup chicken stock
300g/11oz/2¼ cups petits pois
  (baby peas)
juice of 1½ lemons
2 egg yolks
salt and ground black pepper

1 Season the chicken with salt and pepper, then dust generously with flour. Shake off the excess flour; set aside.

2 Heat 15ml/1 tbsp oil in a pan, add the onions, fennel (if using), parsley and fennel seeds. Cook for 3 minutes.

3 Add the remaining oil and the chicken to the pan and cook over a high heat for 5–6 minutes on each side, until lightly browned and cooked through. Remove from the pan and set aside.

4 Deglaze the pan by pouring in the Marsala and cooking over a high heat until reduced to about 30ml/2 tbsp, then pour in the stock. Add the peas and return the chicken and onion mixture to the pan. Cook over a very low heat while you prepare the egg mixture.

5 In a bowl, beat the lemon juice and egg yolks together, then slowly add about 120ml/4fl oz/½ cup of the hot liquid from the chicken and peas, stirring well to combine.

6 Return the mixture to the pan and cook over a low heat, stirring, until the mixture thickens slightly. (Do not allow the mixture to boil or the eggs will curdle and spoil the sauce.) Serve the chicken immediately, sprinkled with a little extra chopped fresh parsley.

Energy 301kcal/1260kJ; Protein 41.6g; Carbohydrate 10.4g, of which sugars 3.3g; Fat 8.4g, of which saturates 1.5g; Cholesterol 105mg; Calcium 34mg; Fibre 4.3g; Sodium 96mg

PAN-FRIED CHICKEN WITH PESTO

WARM PESTO ACCOMPANYING PAN-FRIED CHICKEN MAKES A DELICIOUSLY QUICK MEAL. SERVE WITH BABY CARROTS AND CELERY, BRAISED IN STOCK IN A SEPARATE PAN WHILE THE CHICKEN IS COOKING.

Preparation: 2–3 minutes; Cooking: 18 minutes

SERVES FOUR

INGREDIENTS
15ml/1 tbsp olive oil
4 chicken breast fillets, skinned
fresh basil leaves, to garnish
For the pesto
90ml/6 tbsp olive oil
50g/2oz/½ cup pine nuts
50g/2oz/⅔ cup freshly grated
  Parmesan cheese
50g/2oz/1 cup fresh basil leaves
15g/½oz/¼ cup fresh parsley
2 garlic cloves, crushed
salt and ground black pepper

1 Heat the 15ml/1 tbsp oil in a frying pan. Add the chicken breasts and cook gently for about 15 minutes, turning several times until they are tender, lightly browned and thoroughly cooked.

2 Meanwhile, make the pesto. Place the olive oil, pine nuts, Parmesan cheese, basil leaves, parsley, garlic, and salt and pepper in a food processor and process until smooth and well mixed.

3 Remove the chicken from the pan, cover and keep hot. Reduce the heat slightly, then add the pesto to the pan and cook gently, stirring constantly, for a few minutes, or until the pesto has warmed through.

4 Put the cooked chicken on a plate, pour the warm pesto over the top, then garnish with basil leaves and serve immediately.

Energy 480kcal/1998kJ; Protein 43.2g; Carbohydrate 1g, of which sugars 0.9g; Fat 33.8g, of which saturates 6.4g; Cholesterol 118mg; Calcium 192mg; Fibre 1.1g; Sodium 232mg

CRUMBED CHICKEN WITH GREEN MAYONNAISE

THE CONTRAST BETWEEN CRISP CRUMB AND TENDER CHICKEN IS WHAT MAKES THIS SO SUCCESSFUL.
CAPER MAYONNAISE IS TRADITIONAL BUT MAYO FLAVOURED WITH WASABI WOULD BE GOOD TOO.

Preparation: 4 minutes; Cooking: 12 minutes

SERVES FOUR

INGREDIENTS

4 skinless chicken breast fillets,
  each weighing about 200g/7oz
juice of 1 lemon
5ml/1 tsp paprika
plain (all-purpose) flour,
  for dusting
1–2 eggs
dried breadcrumbs, for coating
about 60ml/4 tbsp olive oil
salt and ground black pepper
lemon wedges (optional), to serve
For the mayonnaise
  120ml/4fl oz/½ cup mayonnaise
  30ml/2 tbsp pickled capers, drained
    and chopped
  30ml/2 tbsp chopped fresh
    parsley

1 Skin the chicken breasts. Lay them on a chopping board, with the outside facing down, and, using a sharp knife, cut through each one horizontally, almost right through, from the rounded edge inwards. Open them up like a book. Press gently, to make a roundish shape the size of a side plate. Sprinkle with lemon juice and paprika.

2 Set out three shallow bowls. Sprinkle flour over one, seasoning it well. Beat the egg with a little salt and pour into the second. Sprinkle the third with dried breadcrumbs.

3 Dip the breasts first into the flour, making sure that it is covered on both sides, then into the egg, then into the breadcrumbs to coat them evenly.

4 Put the mayonnaise ingredients in a bowl and mix well to combine.

5 Heat the oil in a heavy frying pan over a high heat. Fry the breast portions two at a time, turning after 3 minutes, until golden on both sides. Add more oil for the second batch if needed. Serve immediately, with the mayonnaise and lemon wedges, if using.

Energy 582kcal/2428kJ; Protein 51.5g; Carbohydrate 10.3g, of which sugars 0.8g; Fat 37.6g, of which saturates 6g; Cholesterol 210mg; Calcium 43mg; Fibre 0.5g; Sodium 369mg

CHICKEN STUFFED WITH HAM AND CHEESE

A CLASSIC THAT IS PERENNIALLY POPULAR, THIS CONSISTS OF BREASTS OF CHICKEN STUFFED WITH SMOKED HAM AND GRUYÈRE, THEN COATED IN EGG AND BREADCRUMBS AND FRIED UNTIL GOLDEN.

Preparation: 6–8 minutes; Cooking: 10–12 minutes

SERVES FOUR

INGREDIENTS

4 skinless, boneless chicken breasts, about 130g/4½oz each
4 very thin smoked ham slices, halved and rind removed
about 90g/3½oz Gruyère cheese, thinly sliced
plain flour, for coating
2 eggs, beaten
75g/3oz/¾ cup natural-coloured dried breadcrumbs
5ml/1 tsp dried thyme
75g/3oz/6 tbsp butter
60ml/4 tbsp olive oil
salt and ground black pepper
mixed leaf salad, to serve

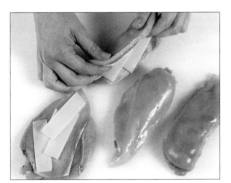

1 Slit the chicken breasts about three-quarters of the way through, then open them up and lay them flat. Place a slice of ham on each cut side of the chicken, trimming to fit if necessary so that the ham does not hang over the edge.

2 Top with the Gruyère slices, making sure that they are well within the ham slices. Fold over the chicken and reshape, pressing well to seal and ensuring that no cheese is visible.

3 Spoon the flour for coating into a shallow bowl. Pour the beaten eggs into another shallow bowl and mix the breadcrumbs with the thyme and seasoning in a third bowl.

4 Toss each stuffed breast in the flour, then coat in egg and breadcrumbs, shaking off any excess.

5 Place half the butter and half the oil in one pan, and the remaining half measures in the other, and heat separately

COOK'S TIP

If you are able to prepare these portions in advance, cover the crumbed breasts and chill them for about 1 hour in the refrigerator to set the coating. It's certainly a tip worth remembering for when you have more time on a recipe.

6 When the fat stops foaming, gently slide in the coated breasts, two in each pan. Shallow fry over a medium-low heat for about 5 minutes each side, turning over carefully with a spatula. Drain on kitchen paper for a few seconds to soak up the excess fat. Serve immediately with the mixed leaf salad.

VARIATION

Instead of Gruyère, try one of the herb-flavoured hard cheeses, such as Double Gloucester with Chives.

Energy 599kcal/2496kJ; Protein 41.8g; Carbohydrate 14.8g, of which sugars 0.8g; Fat 41.5g, of which saturates 18.4g; Cholesterol 220mg; Calcium 222mg; Fibre 0.4g; Sodium 698mg

TURKEY WITH MARSALA CREAM SAUCE

MARSALA MAKES A VERY RICH AND TASTY SAUCE. THE ADDITION OF LEMON JUICE GIVES IT A SHARP EDGE, WHICH HELPS TO OFFSET THE RICHNESS CONTRIBUTED BY THE BUTTER AND CREAM.

Preparation: 6 minutes; Cooking: 12 minutes

SERVES SIX

INGREDIENTS
6 turkey breast steaks
45ml/3 tbsp plain (all-purpose) flour
30ml/2 tbsp olive oil
25g/1oz/2 tbsp butter
60ml/4 tbsp lemon juice
175ml/6fl oz/¾ cup dry Marsala
175ml/6fl oz/¾ cup double
   (heavy) cream
salt and ground black pepper
lemon wedges and chopped fresh
   parsley, to garnish
mangetouts (snow peas) and green
   beans, to serve

1 Put each turkey steak between two sheets of clear film (plastic wrap) and pound with a rolling pin to flatten and stretch the meat. Cut each in half, cutting away and discarding any sinew.

2 Put the flour in a shallow bowl. Season well and coat the meat.

COOK'S TIPS
• You can save a lot of time by cooking the turkey in an electric frying pan, which will hold considerably more pieces than a standard frying pan.
• Cook the mangetouts (snow peas) and beans while the sauce is heating. They will only need a few minutes.

3 Heat the oil and butter in a deep, heavy frying pan until sizzling. Add as many pieces of turkey as the pan will hold and sauté over a medium heat for 2–3 minutes on each side until crispy and tender. Lift the pieces of turkey out with tongs, transfer to a warmed serving dish and keep hot. Repeat with the remaining turkey.

4 Lower the heat. Mix the lemon juice and Marsala together, add to the pan and raise the heat. Bring to the boil, stirring in the sediment, then add the cream. Simmer, stirring constantly, until the sauce is reduced and glossy. Taste for seasoning. Spoon over the turkey, garnish with the lemon wedges and parsley and serve immediately with the mangetouts and green beans.

Energy 326kcal/1355kJ; Protein 25.3g; Carbohydrate 3.5g, of which sugars 1g; Fat 19.9g, of which saturates 12.2g; Cholesterol 106mg; Calcium 26mg; Fibre 0.1g; Sodium 85mg

STIR-FRIED TURKEY WITH BROCCOLI

FOR A DELICIOUS MEAL WITHOUT BREAKING THE BANK, TURKEY IS AN EXCELLENT CHOICE. IT IS RELATIVELY INEXPENSIVE, HAS LITTLE WASTE AND TASTES GREAT IN A STIR-FRY LIKE THIS ONE.

Preparation: 8 minutes; Cooking: 8 minutes

SERVES FOUR

INGREDIENTS

115g/4oz broccoli florets
4 spring onions (scallions)
5ml/1 tsp cornflour (cornstarch)
45ml/3 tbsp oyster sauce
15ml/1 tbsp dark soy sauce
120ml/4fl oz/½ cup chicken stock
10ml/2 tsp lemon juice
45ml/3 tbsp groundnut (peanut) oil
450g/1lb turkey steaks, cut into
   strips about 5mm x 5cm/¼ x 2in
1 small onion, chopped
2 garlic cloves, crushed
10ml/2 tsp grated fresh root ginger
115g/4oz/1½ cups fresh shiitake
   mushrooms, sliced
75g/3oz baby corn, halved
   lengthways
15ml/1 tbsp sesame oil
salt and ground black pepper
egg noodles, to serve

1 Divide the broccoli florets into smaller sprigs and cut the stalks into thin diagonal slices.

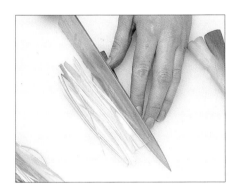

2 Finely chop the white parts of the spring onions and slice the green parts into thin shreds.

3 Put the cornflour in a bowl. Stir in the oyster sauce to make a thin paste, then add the soy sauce, stock and lemon juice. Stir and set aside.

4 Heat a wok until it is hot, add 30ml/ 2 tbsp of the groundnut oil and swirl it around. Add the turkey and stir-fry for about 2 minutes, or until the strips are golden and crispy at the edges, and cooked through. Remove the turkey and keep the pieces warm.

5 Add the remaining groundnut oil to the wok and stir-fry the chopped onion, garlic and ginger over a medium heat for about 1 minute. Increase the heat to high, add the broccoli, mushrooms and corn and stir-fry for 2 minutes.

6 Return the turkey to the wok, then add the cornflour mixture with the chopped spring onion and seasoning. Cook, stirring, for about 1 minute, or until the sauce has thickened. Stir in the sesame oil. Serve immediately on a bed of egg noodles with the finely shredded spring onion sprinkled on top.

COOK'S TIP
For speed and convenience, use straight-to-wok noodles and toss them with the turkey stir-fry until heated through.

Energy 255kcal/1065kJ; Protein 30.3g; Carbohydrate 5.8g, of which sugars 5g; Fat 12.4g, of which saturates 2.4g; Cholesterol 64mg; Calcium 30mg; Fibre 1.7g; Sodium 725mg

SKEWERED DUCK WITH POACHED EGGS

YOU HAVE TO BE ORGANIZED TO MAKE THIS MEAL IN TWENTY MINUTES, BUT IT IS TRULY WORTH THE EFFORT. BOIL THE EGGS IF THAT'S EASIER.

Preparation: 8 minutes; Cooking: 11 minutes

SERVES FOUR

INGREDIENTS

    3 skinless, boneless duck breasts,
      thinly sliced
    30ml/2 tbsp soy sauce
    30ml/2 tbsp balsamic vinegar
    30ml/2 tbsp groundnut oil
    25g/1oz/2 tbsp unsalted butter
    1 shallot, finely chopped
    115g/4oz/1½ cups chanterelle
      mushrooms
    4 eggs
    50g/2oz mixed salad leaves
    salt and ground black pepper
    extra virgin olive oil, to serve

1 Toss the duck in the soy sauce and balsamic vinegar. Cover and marinate for 8–10 minutes. Meanwhile, soak 12 bamboo skewers in water to help prevent them from burning during cooking.

2 Meanwhile, melt the butter in a frying pan and cook the finely chopped shallot until softened but not coloured. Add the chanterelle mushrooms and cook over a high heat for about 5 minutes, stirring occasionally. Leave the pan over a low heat while you cook the duck.

3 Preheat the grill (broiler). Thread the duck slices on to the skewers, pleating them neatly. Place on a grill pan and drizzle with half the oil.

4 Grill (broil) for 3–5 minutes, then turn the skewers and drizzle with the remaining oil. Grill for a further 3 minutes, or until the duck is cooked through and golden.

5 Poach the eggs while the duck is cooking. Half fill a frying pan with water, add salt and heat until simmering. Break the eggs one at a time into a cup before tipping carefully into the water. Poach the eggs gently for about 3 minutes, or until the whites are set. Use a slotted spoon to transfer the eggs to a warm plate and trim off any untidy white.

6 Arrange the salad leaves on serving plates, then add the chanterelles and skewered duck. Carefully add the poached eggs. Drizzle with olive oil and season with ground black pepper, then serve at once.

VARIATION
If you haven't got time to thread the duck strips on to skewers, simply stir-fry in a little oil for a few minutes until crisp and cooked through, then sprinkle over the salad leaves with the mushrooms.

Energy 269kcal/1125kJ; Protein 29.3g; Carbohydrate 1.8g, of which sugars 1.3g; Fat 18.2g, of which saturates 6.3g; Cholesterol 327mg; Calcium 53mg; Fibre 0.7g; Sodium 412mg

GINGERED DUCK WITH TAMARI AND MIRIN

DUCK TAKES VERY LITTLE TIME TO COOK ON A GRIDDLE AND TASTES GREAT WITH A TAMARI AND MIRIN GLAZE. IT LOOKS PRETTY ON ITS BED OF PANCAKES, WITH A DELICATE CUCUMBER GARNISH.

Preparation: 4–5 minutes; Cooking: 13 minutes

SERVES FOUR

INGREDIENTS

4 large duck breast fillets, total
   weight about 675g/1½lb
5cm/2in piece fresh root ginger,
   finely grated
½ large cucumber
12 Chinese pancakes
6 spring onions (scallions),
   finely shredded
For the sauce
   105ml/7 tbsp tamari
   105ml/7 tbsp mirin
   25g/1oz/2 tbsp sugar
   salt and ground black pepper

1 Make four slashes in the skin of each duck breast fillet, then lay them skin-side up on a plate. Squeeze the grated ginger over the duck to extract every drop of juice; discard the pulp. Generously rub the juice all over the duck, especially into the slashes.

2 Peel the cucumber in strips, then cut it in half, scoop out the seeds and chop the flesh. Set aside in a bowl.

3 To make the sauce, mix the tamari, mirin and sugar in a heavy pan and heat gently together until the sugar has dissolved. Increase the heat and simmer for 4–5 minutes, or until the sauce has reduced by about one-third and become syrupy.

4 Heat a griddle on the stove over a high heat until a few drops of water sprinkled on to the surface evaporate instantly. Sear the duck breasts, placing them skin-side down.

5 When the fat has been rendered, and the skin is nicely browned, remove the duck from the pan. Drain off the fat and wipe the pan clean with kitchen paper. Reheat it, return the duck flesh side down, and cook over a medium heat for about 3 minutes.

6 Brush on a little of the sauce, turn the duck over, brush the other side with sauce and turn again. This should take about 1 minute, by which time the duck should be cooked rare – you'll know because, when pressed, there should be some give in the flesh. Remove from the pan and let the duck rest for a few minutes before slicing each breast across at an angle.

7 Meanwhile, wrap the pancakes in foil and warm them in a steamer for about 3 minutes. Serve with the duck, sauce, spring onions and cucumber.

COOK'S TIP
To cook on the barbecue, position the duck on the grill rack over a large drip tray. Cook over hot coals, covered with a lid or tented heavy-duty foil.

Energy 436kcal/1829kJ; Protein 38g; Carbohydrate 23.3g, of which sugars 11g; Fat 21.6g, of which saturates 2.2g; Cholesterol 186mg; Calcium 113mg; Fibre 0.7g; Sodium 1615mg

MEAT

When time is tight, meat often disappears off the agenda entirely. However, it's a myth that meaty main course meals cannot be turned around in minutes. On the contrary, the dishes here include variations on pork, venison, lamb and beef dishes — some well-loved, others less familiar — that simply require a little creative thinking. One of the secrets of quick-cooking meat is to use slender and tender cuts — delicate slices of lamb's liver for example, dainty pork noisettes, or escalopes of veal that can be flattened prior to pan-frying. Many also use diced or minced red meats such as bacon, lamb and beef, often married with herbs or spices such as paprika, oregano or harissa, to produce dishes as diverse as Russian Hamburgers, Corned Beef and Egg Hash or Kofta Lamb Patties. Many of these dishes are served with accompanying dressings and sauces, and suggest simple, sophisticated touches to turn a meal into a showpiece, such as serving buttered tagliatelle on the side of Escalopes of Veal with Cream Sauce. There's even room for a fun party dish or two, such as Mini Ham and Mozzarella Ciabatta Pizzas.

Left: A combination of finely minced (ground) pork and venison makes for rather special sausages — the addition of thyme and onions complements the flavours of the meats perfectly. Despite the sophisticated-sounding main ingredients, this is a very simple recipe that takes no time at all to make.

FRIED PORK <u>WITH</u> SCRAMBLED EGG

WHEN YOU NEED A TASTY MEAL BEFORE GOING OUT FOR THE EVENING, THIS QUICK AND EASY RICE DISH, WITH JUST A LITTLE MEAT, IS THE ANSWER.

Preparation: 5 minutes; Cooking: 12 minutes

SERVES FOUR

INGREDIENTS

- 2 x 250g/9oz sachets quick-cook rice
- 45ml/3 tbsp vegetable oil
- 1 onion, chopped
- 15ml/1 tbsp chopped garlic
- 115g/4oz pork, cut into small cubes
- 2 eggs, beaten
- 30ml/2 tbsp Thai fish sauce
- 15ml/1 tbsp dark soy sauce
- 2.5ml/½ tsp caster (superfine) sugar
- 4 spring onions (scallions), finely sliced, to garnish
- 2 fresh red chillies, sliced, to garnish
- 1 lime, cut into wedges, to garnish

1 Cook the rice according to the instructions on the packet. Spread out and leave to cool.

2 Heat the oil in a wok or large frying pan. Add the onion and garlic and cook for about 2 minutes, until softened.

3 Add the pork to the softened onion and garlic. Stir-fry until the pork changes colour and is cooked.

4 Add the eggs and cook until scrambled into small lumps.

5 Add the rice and continue to stir and toss, to coat it with the oil and prevent it from sticking.

6 Stir in the fish sauce, soy sauce and sugar and mix well. Continue to fry until the rice is thoroughly heated. Spoon into warmed individual bowls and serve, garnished with sliced spring onions, chillies and lime wedges.

Energy 602kcal/2512kJ; Protein 18.8g; Carbohydrate 101.3g, of which sugars 1.1g; Fat 12.8g, of which saturates 2.2g; Cholesterol 113mg; Calcium 45mg; Fibre 0.2g; Sodium 323mg

PORK <u>WITH</u> CREAM <u>AND</u> APPLE SAUCE

TENDER NOISETTES OF PORK IN A CREAMY LEEK AND APPLE SAUCE MAKE A GREAT DINNER PARTY DISH. USE THE SAME WHITE WINE AS THE ONE YOU PLAN TO SERVE WITH THE MEAL, OR TRY CIDER.

Preparation: 2 minutes; Cooking: 18 minutes

SERVES FOUR

INGREDIENTS

30ml/2 tbsp plain (all-purpose) flour
4 noisettes of pork, firmly tied
25g/1oz/2 tbsp butter
4 baby leeks, finely sliced
5ml/1 tsp mustard seeds,
  coarsely crushed
150ml/¼ pint/⅔ cup dry white wine
2 eating apples
150ml/¼ pint/⅔ cup double
  (heavy) cream
30ml/2 tbsp chopped fresh parsley
salt and ground black pepper

1 Place the flour in a bowl and add plenty of seasoning. Turn the noisettes in the flour mixture to coat them lightly.

2 Melt the butter in a heavy frying pan and cook the noisettes for 1 minute on each side.

3 Add the sliced leeks to the pan and cook for 3 minutes. Stir in the mustard seeds. Pour in the wine. Cook gently for 10 minutes, turning the pork occasionally. Peel, core and slice the apples.

VARIATION
Use thin slices of pork fillet (tenderloin) for even faster cooking.

4 Add the sliced apples and double cream and simmer for 3 minutes, or until the pork is fully cooked and the sauce is thick, rich and creamy. Taste for seasoning, then stir in the chopped parsley and serve at once.

Energy 415kcal/1724kJ; Protein 23.1g; Carbohydrate 8.8g, of which sugars 4.4g; Fat 29.5g, of which saturates 17.2g; Cholesterol 128mg; Calcium 45mg; Fibre 1.3g; Sodium 119mg

SPAGHETTI CARBONARA

THIS ITALIAN CLASSIC, FLAVOURED WITH PANCETTA AND A GARLIC AND EGG SAUCE THAT COOKS AROUND THE HOT SPAGHETTI, IS POPULAR WORLDWIDE. IT MAKES A GREAT LAST-MINUTE SUPPER.

Preparation: 3 minutes; Cooking: 15–17 minutes

3 Meanwhile, cook the spaghetti in a large pan of salted boiling water for 10–12 minutes, until just tender.

4 Put the eggs, crème fraîche and grated Parmesan in a bowl. Stir in plenty of black pepper, then beat together well.

5 Drain the pasta thoroughly, tip it into the pan with the pancetta or bacon and toss well to mix.

6 Turn off the heat under the pan, then immediately add the egg mixture and toss thoroughly so that it cooks lightly and coats the pasta.

7 Season to taste, then divide the pasta among four warmed bowls and sprinkle with ground black pepper. Serve immediately, with extra grated Parmesan handed separately.

VARIATION
You can replace the crème fraîche with double (heavy) cream or sour cream, if you prefer.

SERVES FOUR

INGREDIENTS
30ml/2 tbsp olive oil
1 small onion, finely chopped
1 large garlic clove, crushed
8 slices pancetta or rindless smoked streaky (fatty) bacon, cut into 1cm/½in pieces
350g/12oz fresh or dried spaghetti
4 eggs
90–120ml/6–8 tbsp crème fraîche
60ml/4 tbsp freshly grated Parmesan cheese, plus extra to serve
salt and ground black pepper

1 Heat the oil in a large pan, add the onion and garlic and fry gently for about 5 minutes until softened.

2 Add the pancetta or bacon to the pan. Cook for 10 minutes, stirring often.

Energy 708kcal/2966kJ; Protein 30.7g; Carbohydrate 66.6g, of which sugars 4.2g; Fat 37.5g, of which saturates 15.5g; Cholesterol 261mg; Calcium 250mg; Fibre 2.8g; Sodium 824mg

FUSILLI <u>WITH</u> SAUSAGE

GETTING SAUSAGES, PASTA AND TOMATO SAUCE READY AT THE RIGHT MOMENT TAKES A BIT OF JUGGLING, BUT THE RESULT IS A DELICIOUS DISH THAT EVERY MEMBER OF THE FAMILY WILL LOVE.

Preparation: 4–5 minutes; Cooking: 12–15 minutes

SERVES FOUR

INGREDIENTS
    400g/14oz spicy pork sausages
    30ml/2 tbsp olive oil
    1 small onion, finely chopped
    2 garlic cloves, crushed
    1 large yellow (bell) pepper, seeded
      and cut into strips
    5ml/1 tsp paprika
    5ml/1 tsp dried mixed herbs
    5–10ml/1–2 tsp chilli sauce
    400g/14oz can Italian plum tomatoes
    250ml/8fl oz/1 cup vegetable stock
    300g/11oz/2³/₄ cups dried fusilli
    salt and ground black pepper
    freshly grated Pecorino cheese,
      to serve

1 Grill (broil) the sausages for 10–12 minutes until they are browned on all sides.

2 Meanwhile, heat the oil in a large pan, add the onion and garlic and cook for 3 minutes. Add the yellow pepper, paprika, herbs and chilli sauce to taste. Cook for 3 minutes more, stirring occasionally.

3 Pour in the canned tomatoes, breaking them up with a wooden spoon, then add salt and pepper to taste and stir well. Cook over a medium heat for 10–12 minutes, adding the vegetable stock gradually. At the same time, cook the pasta in lightly salted water until tender – about 12–14 minutes.

4 While the tomato sauce and pasta are cooking, drain the cooked sausages on kitchen paper, and, when cool enough to touch, cut each one diagonally into 1cm/½in pieces.

5 Add the sausage pieces to the sauce and mix well. Drain the pasta and add it to the pan of sauce. Toss well, then divide among four warmed bowls, sprinkled with the grated Pecorino.

Energy 709kcal/2970kJ; Protein 20.9g; Carbohydrate 72.2g, of which sugars 10.5g; Fat 39.5g, of which saturates 13.3g; Cholesterol 47mg; Calcium 74mg; Fibre 4.6g; Sodium 774mg

MINI HAM <u>AND</u> MOZZARELLA CIABATTA PIZZAS

IF EVER THERE'S AN ARGUMENT ABOUT WHOSE TURN IT IS TO MAKE LUNCH, VOLUNTEER TO COOK THESE DELICIOUS MINI CIABATTA PIZZAS. THEY'RE PERFECT FOR TAKING ON A PICNIC.

Preparation: 4 minutes; Cooking: 12–15 minutes

SERVES EIGHT

INGREDIENTS
    2 red (bell) peppers
    2 yellow (bell) peppers
    1 loaf ciabatta bread
    8 slices prosciutto or other
      thinly sliced ham, cut into
      thick strips
    150g/5oz mozzarella cheese
    ground black pepper
    tiny basil leaves, to garnish

1 Preheat a grill (broiler). Grill (broil) the peppers, skin sides uppermost, until they are charred. Place them in a bowl, cover and leave for 5 minutes.

2 Cut the bread into eight thick slices and toast both sides until golden.

3 As soon as the roasted peppers are cool enough to touch, remove the skins, cut them into thick strips and arrange them on the toasted bread with the strips of ham.

4 Thinly slice the mozzarella cheese and arrange on top. Grind over plenty of black pepper. Place under the hot grill for 2–3 minutes until the cheese topping is bubbling and golden.

5 Arrange the fresh basil leaves on top and transfer to a serving dish or platter. Leave the cheese to cool for a few minutes, if serving the mini ciabatta pizzas to children.

Energy 154kcal/647kJ; Protein 8.6g; Carbohydrate 18.7g, of which sugars 6.2g; Fat 5.4g, of which saturates 2.9g; Cholesterol 16mg; Calcium 106mg; Fibre 2g; Sodium 325mg

FLAMENCO EGGS

THIS ADAPTABLE DISH IS A SWIRL OF RED, GREEN, YELLOW AND WHITE. YOU CAN USE DIFFERENT VEGETABLES, BUT SHOULD ALWAYS INCLUDE CHORIZO.

Preparation: 4–5 minutes; Cooking: 15 minutes

SERVES FOUR

INGREDIENTS
    30ml/2 tbsp olive oil
    115g/4oz diced smoked bacon
      or pancetta
    2 frying chorizos, cubed
    1 onion, chopped
    2 garlic cloves, finely chopped
    1 red and 1 green (bell) pepper,
      seeded and chopped
    500g/1¼lb tomatoes, chopped
    15–30ml/1–2 tbsp fino sherry
    45ml/3 tbsp chopped parsley
    8 large (US extra large) eggs
    salt, paprika and cayenne pepper
For the garlic crumbs
    4 thick slices stale bread
    oil, for frying
    2 garlic cloves, bruised

1 Preheat the oven to 180°C/350°F/Gas 4. Warm four individual baking dishes.

2 Heat the oil in a large pan and fry the diced bacon and chorizo until they yield their fat. Add the onion and garlic and cook gently until softened, stirring.

3 Add the peppers and tomatoes and cook to reduce, stirring occasionally. Add some paprika and stir in the sherry.

COOK'S TIP
The chorizo and vegetable mixture mustn't be too dry, so add a little more sherry if necessary.

4 Divide the vegetable mixture evenly among the baking dishes. Sprinkle with parsley. Swirl the eggs together with a fork (without overmixing) and season well with salt and cayenne. Pour over the vegetable mixture.

5 Bake the eggs and vegetables for 8 minutes, or until the eggs are just set.

6 Meanwhile make the garlic crumbs. Cut the crusts off the bread and reduce to crumbs in a food processor, or use a hand grater.

7 Heat plenty of oil in a large frying pan over a high heat, add the garlic cloves for a few moments to flavour it, then remove and discard them. Throw in the breadcrumbs and brown quickly, scooping them out on to kitchen paper with a slotted spoon. Season with a little salt and paprika, then sprinkle them around the edge of the eggs, when ready to serve.

Energy 597kcal/2485kJ; Protein 27.3g; Carbohydrate 28g, of which sugars 11.1g; Fat 42.4g, of which saturates 11.7g; Cholesterol 429mg; Calcium 163mg; Fibre 3.2g; Sodium 1116mg

HOME-MADE PORK AND VENISON SAUSAGES

VENISON SAUSAGES HAVE AN EXCELLENT FLAVOUR, A MUCH LOWER FAT CONTENT THAN MOST SAUSAGES AND THEY'RE EASY TO MAKE IF YOU FORGET ABOUT SAUSAGE SKINS AND JUST SHAPE THE MIXTURE.

Preparation: 5 minutes; Cooking: 12 minutes

MAKES 1.4KG/3LB

INGREDIENTS
900g/2lb finely minced
   (ground) venison
450g/1lb finely minced
   (ground) belly of pork
15ml/1 tbsp salt
10ml/2 tsp ground black pepper
1 garlic clove, crushed
5ml/1 tsp dried thyme
1 egg, beaten
plain (all-purpose) flour, for dusting
oil, for frying
fried onions, grilled (broiled)
   tomatoes and field (portabello)
   mushrooms, to serve

1 Combine all the sausage ingredients, except the flour and oil, in a bowl. Take a small piece of the mixture and fry it in a little oil in a heavy frying pan, then taste to check the seasoning for the batch. Adjust if necessary.

2 Using floured hands, roll the mixture into slender sausages.

3 Heat the oil in a large, heavy frying pan and shallow-fry the sausages for 10 minutes or until they are golden brown and cooked right through.

4 If you use a large pan, you'll be able to fry some onion rings alongside the sausages. At the same time, grill (broil) mushrooms and halved tomatoes to serve on the side.

COOK'S TIP
If you find yourself with more sausages than you need for one meal, freeze the surplus in an airtight container for no more than a month. Be sure to thaw the sausages completely before cooking.

Energy 1747kcal/7356kJ; Protein 302.4g; Carbohydrate 0g, of which sugars 0g; Fat 65.3g, of which saturates 17.6g; Cholesterol 924mg; Calcium 105mg; Fibre 0g; Sodium 880mg

PORK <u>ON</u> LEMON GRASS STICKS

THESE MAKE A SUBSTANTIAL SNACK, EITHER ON THEIR OWN OR AS PART OF A BARBECUE MENU. THE LEMON GRASS STICKS NOT ONLY ADD A SUBTLE FLAVOUR BUT ARE ALSO A GOOD TALKING POINT.

Preparation: 6 minutes; Cooking: 6−8 minutes

SERVES FOUR

INGREDIENTS

  300g/11oz/1½ cups minced
    (ground) pork
  4 garlic cloves, crushed
  4 fresh coriander (cilantro) roots,
    finely chopped
  2.5ml/½ tsp granulated sugar
  15ml/1 tbsp soy sauce
  salt and ground black pepper
  8 x 10cm/4in lengths lemon
    grass stalk
  sweet chilli sauce, to serve

VARIATION

Slimmer versions of these pork sticks are perfect for parties. The mixture will be enough for 12 lemon grass sticks if you use it sparingly.

1 Place the minced pork, crushed garlic, chopped coriander root, sugar and soy sauce in a large bowl. Season with salt and pepper to taste and mix well.

2 Divide into eight portions and mould each one into a ball. It may help to dampen your hands before shaping the mixture, to prevent it from sticking.

3 Stick a length of lemon grass halfway into each ball, then press the meat mixture around the lemon grass to make a shape like a chicken leg.

4 Cook the pork sticks under a hot grill (broiler) for 3–4 minutes on each side, until golden and cooked through. Serve with the chilli sauce for dipping.

Energy 132kcal/552kJ; Protein 14.7g; Carbohydrate 2g, of which sugars 1.6g; Fat 7.3g, of which saturates 2.7g; Cholesterol 50mg; Calcium 10mg; Fibre 0.2g; Sodium 317mg

DEVILLED KIDNEYS ON BRIOCHE CROÛTES

THE TRICK WITH LAMB'S KIDNEYS IS NOT TO OVERCOOK THEM, SO THIS RECIPE IS A GIFT FOR THE QUICK COOK. CREAM TAMES THE FIERY SAUCE, MAKING A MIXTURE THAT TASTES GREAT ON CROÛTES.

Preparation: 5 minutes; Cooking: 12–14 minutes

SERVES FOUR

INGREDIENTS
- 8 mini brioche slices
- 25g/1oz/2 tbsp butter
- 1 shallot, finely chopped
- 2 garlic cloves, finely chopped
- 115g/4oz/1½ cups mushrooms, halved
- 1.5ml/¼ tsp cayenne pepper
- 15ml/1 tbsp Worcestershire sauce
- 8 lamb's kidneys, halved and trimmed
- 150ml/¼ pint/⅔ cup double (heavy) cream
- 30ml/2 tbsp chopped fresh parsley

1 Preheat the grill (broiler) and toast the brioche slices until golden brown on both sides. Keep warm.

2 Melt the butter in a frying pan. Add the shallot, garlic and mushrooms and cook for 5 minutes, or until the shallot has softened. Stir in the cayenne pepper and Worcestershire sauce and simmer for 1 minute.

3 Add the kidneys to the pan and cook for 3–5 minutes on each side. Finally, stir in the cream and simmer for about 2 minutes, or until the sauce has heated through and has thickened slightly.

4 Remove the brioche croûtes from the wire rack and place on warmed plates. Top with the kidneys. Sprinkle with chopped parsley and serve immediately.

COOK'S TIPS
If you can't find mini brioches, you can use a large brioche instead. Slice it thickly and stamp out croûtes using a 5cm/2in round cutter. If you prefer, the brioche croûtes can be fried rather than toasted. Melt 25g/1oz/2 tbsp butter in a frying pan and fry the croûtes until crisp and golden on both sides.

Energy 575kcal/2412kJ; Protein 37.7g; Carbohydrate 40.7g, of which sugars 13.2g; Fat 30.3g, of which saturates 16.3g; Cholesterol 623mg; Calcium 122mg; Fibre 2g; Sodium 599mg

KOFTA LAMB PATTIES

FOR A QUICK AND EASY SUPPER, SIMPLY SLIDE THESE SPICY LITTLE PATTIES INTO CONES MADE BY ROLLING WARMED TORTILLAS. A DOLLOP OF THICK YOGURT OR CRÈME FRAÎCHE WOULDN'T GO AMISS.

Preparation: 8 minutes; Cooking: 10 minutes

SERVES FOUR

INGREDIENTS
    450g/1lb minced (ground) lamb
    1–2 large slices French bread,
      very finely crumbed
    ½ bunch fresh coriander (cilantro),
      finely chopped
    5 garlic cloves, chopped
    1 onion, finely chopped
    juice of ½ lemon
    5ml/1 tsp ground cumin
    5ml/1 tsp paprika
    15ml/1 tbsp curry powder
    a pinch each of ground cardamom,
      turmeric and cinnamon
    15ml/1 tbsp tomato purée (paste)
    cayenne pepper or chopped fresh
      chillies (optional)
    1 egg, beaten (optional)
    salt and ground black pepper
    flat bread and salads, to serve

1 Put the lamb, crumbed bread, coriander, garlic, onion, lemon juice, spices, tomato purée, cayenne pepper or chillies and seasoning in a large bowl. Mix well. If the mixture does not bind together, add the beaten egg and a little more bread.

2 With wet hands, shape the mixture into four large or eight small patties.

3 Heat a heavy non-stick frying pan, add the patties and cook for about 10 minutes, until browned. Turn once or twice, but make sure that they do not fall apart. Serve hot with flat bread and salads.

VARIATION
Mix a handful of raisins or sultanas (golden raisins) into the meat mixture before shaping it into patties.

Energy 298kcal/1249kJ; Protein 24.2g; Carbohydrate 16.5g, of which sugars 2.6g; Fat 15.5g, of which saturates 7.1g; Cholesterol 87mg; Calcium 57mg; Fibre 1.1g; Sodium 242mg

FRIED LAMB MEATBALLS

MEATBALLS COOK QUICKLY; THE FIDDLY BIT IS SHAPING THEM. MIXING EVERYTHING TOGETHER WITH YOUR HANDS IS VERY SATISFYING AND WILL HELP SPEED UP THE PROCESS TOO.

Preparation: 10–15 minutes; Cooking: 5 minutes

SERVES FOUR

INGREDIENTS
  2 medium slices of bread,
    crusts removed
  1 onion
  500g/1¼lb minced (ground) lamb
    or beef
  5ml/1 tsp each dried thyme
    and oregano
  45ml/3 tbsp chopped fresh flat leaf
    parsley, plus extra to garnish
  1 egg, lightly beaten
  salt and ground black pepper
  lemon wedges, to serve (optional)
For frying
  25g/1oz/¼ cup plain
    (all-purpose) flour
  30–45ml/2–3 tbsp vegetable oil

1 Soak the slices of bread in a shallow bowl of water for 5 minutes. While the bread is soaking, grate or very finely chop the onion.

2 Drain the bread. Using clean hands, squeeze it dry and put it in a large bowl. Add the meat, onion, dried herbs, parsley, egg, salt and pepper to the bread. Mix together, preferably using your hands, until well blended.

3 Shape the meat mixture into individual balls about the size of a walnut, and roll them in the flour to give them a light dusting, shaking off any excess coating.

4 Heat the oil in a large frying pan. When it is hot, add the meatballs and fry for about 5 minutes, turning them frequently, until they are cooked through and look crisp and brown.

5 Using a slotted spoon, lift out the meatballs and drain on a double sheet of kitchen paper, to get rid of the excess oil. Sprinkle with the remaining chopped parsley and serve with lemon wedges, if you like.

Energy 411kcal/1710kJ; Protein 28.4g; Carbohydrate 13g, of which sugars 1.5g; Fat 27.6g, of which saturates 9.7g; Cholesterol 123mg; Calcium 66mg; Fibre 1.1g; Sodium 192mg

PITTAS WITH SPICED LAMB KOFTAS

WHEN YOU ARE EATING AL FRESCO, A BITE IN THE HAND IS WORTH TWO ON THE PLATE. HARISSA GIVES THE LAMB KOFTAS A MILDLY FIERY FLAVOUR, EASILY TAMED BY A TRICKLE OF YOGURT.

Preparation: 10 minutes; Cooking: 10 minutes

SERVES FOUR

INGREDIENTS
  450g/1lb/2 cups minced
    (ground) lamb
  1 small onion, finely chopped
  10ml/2 tsp harissa paste
  8 pitta breads, salad vegetables,
    mint and yogurt, to serve
  salt and ground black pepper

1 Prepare a barbecue. Soak eight wooden skewers in cold water for 10 minutes.

2 Meanwhile, put the lamb in a large bowl and add the onion and harissa. Mix well to combine, and season with plenty of salt and pepper.

VARIATION
Instead of adding mint leaves and yogurt separately to the pittas, spoon in some tzatziki, made by mixing finely diced cucumber, spring onions (scallions) and crushed garlic with Greek (US strained plain) yogurt.

3 Divide the mixture into eight equal pieces and press on to the skewers in a sausage shape to make the koftas.

4 Cook the skewered koftas for about 10 minutes, turning occasionally, until cooked through.

5 Warm the pitta breads on the barbecue grill, then split. Place a kofta in each one, and remove the skewer. Add some cucumber and tomato slices, mint leaves and a drizzle of natural (plain) yogurt.

Energy 609kcal/2568kJ; Protein 35.3g; Carbohydrate 83.8g, of which sugars 5.4g; Fat 17g, of which saturates 7.3g; Cholesterol 87mg; Calcium 230mg; Fibre 3.8g; Sodium 737mg

ESCALOPES OF VEAL WITH CREAM SAUCE

THIS QUICK, EASY DISH IS DELICIOUS SERVED WITH BUTTERED TAGLIATELLE AND LIGHTLY STEAMED GREEN VEGETABLES. IT WORKS JUST AS WELL WITH TURKEY ESCALOPES.

Preparation: 2–3 minutes; Cooking: 15–17 minutes

SERVES FOUR

INGREDIENTS

15ml/1 tbsp plain flour
4 veal escalopes (scallops),
    about 75–115g/3–4oz each
30ml/2 tbsp sunflower oil
1 shallot, chopped
150g/5oz/2 cups oyster
    mushrooms, sliced
30ml/2 tbsp Marsala or
    medium-dry sherry
200ml/7fl oz/scant 1 cup crème
    fraîche or sour cream
30ml/2 tbsp chopped fresh tarragon
salt and ground black pepper

COOK'S TIP
If they are too thick, flatten the escalopes (scallops) with a rolling pin. It'll help to cut down the cooking time.

1 Season the flour and use to dust the veal, then set the meat aside.

2 Heat the oil in a large frying pan and cook the shallot and mushrooms for 5 minutes. Add the escalopes and cook over a high heat for about 1½ minutes on each side. Pour in the Marsala or sherry and cook until reduced by half.

3 Use a spatula to remove the veal escalopes from the pan. Stir the crème fraîche, tarragon and seasoning into the juices remaining in the pan and simmer gently for 3–5 minutes, or until the sauce is thick and creamy.

4 Return the escalopes to the pan and heat through for 1 minute before serving.

Energy 377kcal/1567kJ; Protein 25.1g; Carbohydrate 5.9g, of which sugars 2.5g; Fat 27.5g, of which saturates 14.9g; Cholesterol 108mg; Calcium 45mg; Fibre 0.8g; Sodium 75mg

VEAL WITH ANCHOVIES AND MOZZARELLA

SCALOPPINE ARE THIN ESCALOPES OF VEAL CUT ACROSS THE GRAIN. FOR THIS DISH, THEY ARE ROLLED AROUND A RICH ANCHOVY, TOMATO AND MOZZARELLA FILLING AND SERVED WITH A MARSALA SAUCE.

Preparation: 6 minutes; Cooking: 12 minutes

SERVES SIX

INGREDIENTS
50g/2oz/¼ cup unsalted
  (sweet) butter
50g/2oz can anchovies
4 fresh tomatoes, peeled
  and chopped
30ml/2 tbsp chopped fresh flat
  leaf parsley
6 veal escalopes (scallops), about
  100g/3¾oz each
200g/7oz mozzarella cheese, cut in
  thin slices
30ml/2 tbsp olive oil
175ml/6fl oz/¾ cup Marsala or
  medium dry sherry
30–45ml/2–3 tbsp whipping cream
salt and ground black pepper
fresh herbs, to garnish
cooked pasta, to serve

VARIATIONS
For a more defined flavour, try smoked mozzarella, Provolone or Bel Paese instead of regular mozzarella. If you prefer not to eat veal, substitute thinly sliced pork escalopes or turkey steaks. They will cook in roughly the same amount of time.

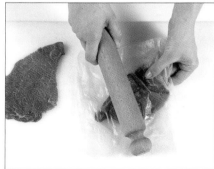

1 Melt half the butter in a small pan. Drain the anchovies and add them to the pan. Cook gently, stirring with a wooden spoon, until they break down to a pulp. Stir in the tomatoes and cook for about 3 minutes until they have softened and reduced. Transfer to a bowl, cool, then stir in the parsley.

2 Place each veal escalope in turn between two sheets of baking parchment and beat with a mallet or rolling pin until thin. Spread the escalopes out on a board and sprinkle with ground black pepper. Divide the anchovy and tomato mixture among them, leaving the edges free.

3 Top with the slices of cheese. Fold the long edges of each escalope towards the centre, then bring up the sides to form a neat parcel. Secure with kitchen string or cocktail sticks (toothpicks).

4 Heat the remaining butter with the oil in a large frying pan. Brown the rolled escalopes, then pour in the Marsala or sherry. Cook, uncovered, for 5 minutes or until the Marsala or sherry has reduced and thickened.

5 Transfer the rolls to a serving plate, stir the pan juices to incorporate any sediment, then pour in the cream. Reheat without boiling, then strain over the rolls. Garnish with fresh herbs and serve with tagliatelle, linguine or any other flat ribbon noodles.

Energy 367kcal/1529kJ; Protein 31.7g; Carbohydrate 4g, of which sugars 4g; Fat 22g, of which saturates 11.5g; Cholesterol 100mg; Calcium 161mg; Fibre 0.7g; Sodium 584mg

VEAL WITH LEMON

POPULAR IN ITALIAN RESTAURANTS, THIS DISH IS VERY SIMPLE TO MAKE AT HOME. WHITE VERMOUTH AND LEMON JUICE MAKE THE PERFECT SAUCE FOR THE DELICATELY FLAVOURED MEAT.

Preparation: 3–4 minutes; Cooking: 15 minutes

SERVES FOUR

INGREDIENTS

4 veal escalopes (scallops)
30–45ml/2–3 tbsp plain
  (all-purpose) flour
50g/2oz/¼ cup butter
60ml/4 tbsp olive oil
60ml/4 tbsp Italian dry white
  vermouth or dry white wine
45ml/3 tbsp lemon juice
salt and ground black pepper
lemon wedges, grated lemon rind
  and fresh parsley, to garnish
salad, to serve

VARIATIONS
• Use skinless boneless chicken breast portions instead of the veal. If they are thick, cut them in half before pounding.
• Substitute thin slices of pork fillet (tenderloin) for the veal and use orange juice instead of lemon.

1 Put each veal escalope between two sheets of clear film (plastic wrap) and pound with the side of a rolling pin or the smooth side of a meat mallet until the slices are very thin.

2 Cut the pounded escalopes in half or quarters. Season the flour with a little salt and pepper and use it to coat the escalopes on both sides. Shake off any excess seasoned flour.

3 Melt the butter with half the oil in a large, heavy frying pan until sizzling. Add as many escalopes as the pan will hold. Cook over a medium to high heat for about 2 minutes on each side until lightly coloured. Remove with a spatula and keep hot. Add the remaining oil to the pan and cook the remaining veal escalopes in the same way.

4 Remove the pan from the heat and add the vermouth or wine and the lemon juice. Stir vigorously to mix well with the pan juices, then return the pan to the heat.

5 Return all the veal escalopes to the pan. Spoon the sauce over to coat the veal. Heat through for about 2 minutes, shaking the pan occasionally. Serve immediately, garnished with lemon wedges, lemon rind and a sprinkling of parsley.

Energy 360kcal/1498kJ; Protein 29g; Carbohydrate 4.8g, of which sugars 0.6g; Fat 23.5g, of which saturates 8.9g; Cholesterol 92mg; Calcium 16mg; Fibre 0.2g; Sodium 151mg

CALF'S LIVER WITH CRISP ONIONS

SAUTÉED OR CREAMY MASHED POTATOES GO WELL WITH FRIED CALF'S LIVER. SERVE WITH A SALAD OF MIXED LEAVES AND FRESH HERBS, TO COMPLEMENT THE SIMPLE FLAVOURS OF THIS MAIN COURSE.

Preparation: 3–4 minutes; Cooking: 16 minutes

SERVES FOUR

INGREDIENTS

50g/2oz/¼ cup butter
4 onions, thinly sliced
5ml/1 tsp caster (superfine) sugar
4 slices calf's liver, each weighing
  about 115g/4oz
30ml/2 tbsp plain (all-purpose) flour
30ml/2 tbsp olive oil
salt and ground black pepper
parsley, to garnish

1 Melt the butter in a large, heavy-based pan with a lid. Add the onions and mix well to coat with butter. Cover the pan with a tight-fitting lid and cook gently for 10 minutes, stirring occasionally.

2 Stir in the sugar and cover the pan. Cook the onions for 8 minutes more, or until they are soft and golden. Increase the heat, remove the lid and stir the onions over a high heat until they are deep gold and crisp. Use a slotted spoon to remove the onions from the pan, draining off the fat.

3 Meanwhile, rinse the calf's liver in cold water and pat it dry on kitchen paper. Season the flour, put it on a plate and turn the slices of liver in it until they are lightly coated in flour.

COOK'S TIP
Take care not to cook the liver for too long as this may cause it to toughen.

4 Heat the oil in a large frying pan, add the liver and cook for about 2 minutes on each side, or until lightly browned and just firm. Arrange the liver on warmed plates, with the crisp onions. Garnish with parsley and serve with sautéed or mashed potatoes.

Energy 315kcal/1310kJ; Protein 22.7g; Carbohydrate 11.8g, of which sugars 4.4g; Fat 19.9g, of which saturates 8.5g; Cholesterol 452mg; Calcium 39mg; Fibre 1.3g; Sodium 160mg

CORNED BEEF AND EGG HASH

THIS IS TRADITIONAL FAMILY FARE AT ITS VERY BEST. WARM AND COMFORTING, AND MADE IN
MINUTES, IT WILL BECOME A FIRM FAVOURITE VERY QUICKLY.

Preparation: 4–5 minutes; Cooking: 12–15 minutes

SERVES FOUR

INGREDIENTS

  30ml/2 tbsp vegetable oil
  25g/1oz/2 tbsp butter
  1 onion, finely chopped
  1 green (bell) pepper, seeded
   and diced
  2 large firm boiled potatoes, diced
  350g/12oz can corned beef, cubed
  1.5ml/¼ tsp grated nutmeg
  1.5ml/¼ tsp paprika
  4 eggs
  salt and ground black pepper
  parsley, deep-fried in oil, to garnish
  sweet chilli sauce or tomato sauce,
   to serve

COOK'S TIP
Put the can of corned beef into the
refrigerator to chill for about half an hour
before using – it will firm up and be
much easier to cut into cubes.

1 Heat the oil and butter together in a
large frying pan. Add the onion and fry
for 3–4 minutes until softened.

2 In a bowl, mix together the green
pepper, potatoes, corned beef, nutmeg
and paprika. Season well. Add to the
pan and toss gently to distribute the
cooked onion. Press down lightly and
fry without stirring on a medium heat for
about 3–4 minutes until a golden brown
crust has formed on the underside.

3 Stir the mixture through to distribute
the crust, then repeat the frying twice,
until the mixture is well browned.

4 Make four wells in the hash and
carefully crack an egg into each. Cover
and cook gently for about 4–5 minutes
until the egg whites are set.

5 Sprinkle with deep-fried parsley and
cut into quarters. Serve hot with sweet
chilli sauce or tomato sauce.

Energy 421kcal/1758kJ; Protein 30.9g; Carbohydrate 17g, of which sugars 5.4g; Fat 26.2g, of which saturates 10.6g; Cholesterol 277mg; Calcium 65mg; Fibre 1.7g; Sodium 871mg

STEAK CIABATTA WITH HUMMUS AND SALAD

*PACKED WITH GARLICKY HUMMUS AND A MUSTARD-SEASONED DRESSING ON THE CRUNCHY SALAD,
THESE STEAK SANDWICHES ARE JUST RIGHT FOR LUNCH ON THE PATIO.*

Preparation: 5 minutes; Cooking: 6–9 minutes

SERVES FOUR

INGREDIENTS

   3 garlic cloves, crushed to a
     paste with enough salt to season
     the steaks
   30ml/2 tbsp extra virgin olive oil
   4 sirloin steaks, 2.5cm/1in thick,
     total weight about 900g/2lb
   2 romaine lettuce hearts
   4 small ciabatta breads
   salt and ground black pepper
For the dressing
   10ml/2 tsp Dijon mustard
   5ml/1 tsp cider or white wine vinegar
   15ml/1 tbsp olive oil
For the hummus
   400g/14oz can chickpeas, drained
     and rinsed
   45ml/3 tbsp tahini
   2 garlic cloves, crushed
   juice of 1 lemon
   30ml/2 tbsp water

1 To make the hummus, place the chickpeas in a large bowl and mash to a paste. Add the tahini, garlic, lemon juice, salt and pepper. Stir in the water. Mash together well.

2 Make a dressing by mixing the mustard and vinegar in a jar. Add the oil and season to taste. Shake well.

3 Mix the garlic and oil in a dish. Add the steaks and rub the mixture into both surfaces.

4 Preheat the grill (broiler). Cook the steaks on a rack in a grill pan. For rare meat, allow 2 minutes on one side and 3 minutes on the second side. For medium steaks, allow 4 minutes on each side. Transfer to a plate, cover and rest for 2 minutes.

5 Dress the lettuce. Split each ciabatta and heat on the grill rack for a minute. Fill with hummus, the steaks and leaves. Cut each in half and serve immediately, just as they are.

Energy 765kcal/3210kJ; Protein 69.8g; Carbohydrate 55.2g, of which sugars 2.8g; Fat 30.8g, of which saturates 7.4g; Cholesterol 115mg; Calcium 222mg; Fibre 6.7g; Sodium 783mg

RUSSIAN HAMBURGERS

THESE TASTY HAMBURGERS CAN BE MADE VERY QUICKLY AND YET STILL TASTE DIVINE.
SERVE THEM SOLO, WITH SAUCE, OR JUST SLIDE THEM INTO BUNS.

Preparation: 6 minutes; Cooking: 12–14 minutes

SERVES FOUR

INGREDIENTS
  2 thick slices white bread,
    crusts removed
  45ml/3 tbsp milk
  450g/1lb finely minced (ground)
    beef, lamb or veal
  1 egg, beaten
  30ml/2 tbsp plain (all-purpose) flour
  30ml/2 tbsp sunflower oil
  salt and ground black pepper
  tomato sauce, pickled vegetables and
    crispy fried onions, to serve

VARIATION
These burgers are quite plain. For extra
flavour, add freshly grated nutmeg to
the mixture, or a little chopped onion
fried in oil.

1 Cut the bread into chunks and crumb
in a food processor, or by using a metal
grater. Put the breadcrumbs in a bowl
and spoon over the milk. Leave to soak
for 3 minutes.

2 Add the minced meat, egg, salt and
pepper and mix all the ingredients
together thoroughly.

3 Divide the mixture into four equal
portions and shape into ovals, each
about 10cm/4in long and 5cm/2in wide.
Coat each with the flour.

4 Heat the oil in a frying pan and fry the
burgers for 6–7 minutes on each side.
Serve with a tomato sauce, pickled
vegetables and fried onions.

Energy 384kcal/1597kJ; Protein 26g; Carbohydrate 13g, of which sugars 1g; Fat 25.7g, of which saturates 9g; Cholesterol 116mg; Calcium 56mg; Fibre 0.4g; Sodium 183mg

BEEF STROGANOFF

THIS IS ONE OF THE MOST FAMOUS FAST MEAT DISHES, CONSISTING OF TENDER STRIPS OF STEAK IN A
TANGY SOUR CREAM SAUCE. SERVE IT WITH POTATO FRIES, AS HERE, OR WITH NOODLES.

Preparation: 3 minutes; Cooking: 12 minutes

SERVES FOUR

INGREDIENTS
  450g/1lb fillet steak (beef tenderloin)
    or rump steak, trimmed and
    tenderized with a rolling pin or
    meat mallet
  15ml/1 tbsp sunflower oil
  25g/1oz/2 tbsp butter
  1 onion, sliced
  15ml/1 tbsp plain (all-purpose) flour
  5ml/1 tsp tomato purée (paste)
  5ml/1 tsp Dijon mustard
  5ml/1 tsp lemon juice
  150ml/¼ pint/⅔ cup soured cream
  salt and ground black pepper
  fresh herbs, to garnish

1 Using a sharp cook's knife, cut the
tenderized steak into thin strips, about
5cm/2in long. Heat the oil and half the
butter in a frying pan and fry the beef
over a high heat for 2 minutes, or until
browned. Remove with a slotted spoon,
leaving any juices behind.

2 Melt the remaining butter in the pan
and gently fry the onion for 8 minutes,
until soft. Stir in the flour, tomato purée,
mustard, lemon juice and sour cream.
Return the beef to the pan and stir until
the sauce is bubbling. Season well and
garnish with fresh herbs.

Energy 308kcal/1282kJ; Protein 26.5g; Carbohydrate 5.8g, of which sugars 2.5g; Fat 20.1g, of which saturates 10.2g; Cholesterol 102mg; Calcium 50mg; Fibre 0.4g; Sodium 124mg

MEXICAN TACOS

READY-MADE TACO SHELLS MAKE PERFECT EDIBLE CONTAINERS FOR SHREDDED SALAD, MEAT FILLINGS, GRATED CHEESE AND SOUR CREAM. THIS IS A SUPER SUPPER THAT SPARES THE COOK HARD LABOUR.

Preparation: 5 minutes; Cooking: 10–12 minutes

SERVES FOUR

INGREDIENTS

15ml/1 tbsp olive oil
250g/9oz lean minced (ground) beef or turkey
2 garlic cloves, crushed
5ml/1 tsp ground cumin
5–10ml/1–2 tsp mild chilli powder
8 ready-made taco shells
½ small iceberg lettuce, shredded
1 small onion, thinly sliced
2 tomatoes, chopped in chunks
1 avocado, halved, stoned (pitted) and sliced
60ml/4 tbsp sour cream
125g/4oz/1 cup grated Cheddar or Monterey Jack cheese
salt and ground black pepper

1 Heat the oil in a frying pan. Add the meat, with the garlic and spices, and brown over a medium heat, stirring frequently to break up any lumps. Season, cook for 10 minutes, then set aside to cool slightly.

2 Meanwhile, warm the taco shells according to the instructions on the packet. Do not let them get too crisp.

3 Spoon the lettuce, onion, tomatoes and avocado slices into the taco shells. Top with the sour cream followed by the minced beef or turkey mixture.

COOK'S TIP
Stir-fried strips of turkey, chicken or pork are excellent instead of the minced beef.

4 Sprinkle the grated Cheddar or Monterey Jack cheese into the tacos and serve immediately, just as the cheese is melting. Tacos are eaten with the fingers and there's usually a certain amount of fallout, so have plenty of paper napkins handy.

HOME-MADE BURGERS <u>WITH</u> RELISH

MAKING YOUR OWN BURGERS MEANS YOU CONTROL WHAT GOES INTO THEM. THESE ARE FULL OF FLAVOUR AND ALWAYS PROVE POPULAR. THE TANGY RATATOUILLE RELISH IS VERY EASY TO MAKE.

Preparation: 6 minutes; Cooking: 14 minutes

SERVES FOUR

INGREDIENTS
  2 shallots, chopped
  450g/1lb lean minced (ground) beef
  30ml/2 tbsp chopped parsley
  30ml/2 tbsp tomato ketchup
  1 garlic clove, crushed
  1 fresh green chilli, finely chopped
    and seeded
  15ml/1 tbsp olive oil
  400g/14oz can ratatouille
  4 burger buns
  lettuce leaves
  salt and ground black pepper, to taste

1 Put the shallots in a bowl with boiling water to cover. Leave for 1–2 minutes, then slip off the skins and chop the shallots finely.

2 Mix half the shallots with the beef in a bowl. Add the chopped parsley and tomato ketchup, with salt and pepper to taste. Mix well with clean hands. Divide the mixture into four. Knead each portion into a ball, then flatten it into a burger.

3 Make a spicy relish by cooking the remaining shallot with the garlic and green chilli in the olive oil for 2–3 minutes, until softened.

4 Add the canned ratatouille to the pan containing the vegetables. Bring to the boil, then simmer for 5 minutes.

VARIATION
Set these burgers on individual plates with spicy corn relish on the side. To make the relish, heat 30ml/2 tbsp oil in a pan and fry 1 onion, 2 crushed garlic cloves and 1 seeded red chilli until soft. Add 10ml/2 tsp garam masala and cook for 2 minutes, then mix in a 320g/11¼oz can whole kernel corn and the grated rind and juice of 1 lime.

5 Meanwhile, preheat the grill (broiler) and cook the burgers for about 5 minutes on each side, until browned and cooked through. Meanwhile, split the burger buns. Arrange lettuce leaves on the bun bases, add the burgers and top with warm relish and the bun tops.

Energy 484kcal/2021kJ; Protein 27.9g; Carbohydrate 30.2g, of which sugars 7.7g; Fat 28.8g, of which saturates 9.3g; Cholesterol 68mg; Calcium 120mg; Fibre 2.2g; Sodium 473mg

VEGETARIAN

While these main course dishes will hold boundless appeal for vegetarians seeking new inspiriation, they will be just as loved by meat-eaters for their colour and crunch, or melt-in-the-mouth creaminess. Wholesome grains such as pasta, couscous and rice provide the perfect contrast to succulent vegetables, while eggs and dairy are put to exceptional use as well. Spinach and soft cheese, for example, make a heavenly match in the topping for Fiorentina Pizza, while Sweet Peppers stuffed with ricotta and mozzarella are a summer barbecue favourite. The addition of egg creates two superb variations on the omelette theme: a soufflé-style recipe using mushrooms, and a vegetable-laden Spicy Omelette made with chillies, morsels of potato, corn and peas. For those seeking lower-fat alternatives, Tofu and Pepper Kebabs substitute dairy for the creaminess of firm tofu, while the heartier Creamy Leek Casserole or Mushroom Stroganoff are unbeatable comfort fare, perfect for winter evening suppers.

Left: Coating creamy tofu in ground roasted peanuts gives these colourful kebabs extra crunch, as well as a spicy-salty kick. They can be cooked over a barbecue, or under a foil-lined grill (broiler), and are best served with a dipping sauce.

SPAGHETTI WITH LEMON

THIS IS THE DISH TO MAKE WHEN YOU RUSH HOME FOR A QUICK BITE TO EAT AND FIND THERE'S NOTHING IN THE HOUSE EXCEPT A LEMON, SOME GARLIC AND WHAT'S IN THE PANTRY.

Preparation: 2–3 minutes; Cooking: 15 minutes

SERVES FOUR

INGREDIENTS
    350g/12oz dried spaghetti
    90ml/6 tbsp extra virgin olive oil
    juice of 1 large lemon
    2 garlic cloves, cut into
        very thin slivers
    salt and ground black pepper

COOK'S TIP
Spaghetti is the best type of pasta for this recipe, because the olive oil and lemon juice cling to its long thin strands. If you are out of spaghetti, use another dried long pasta shape instead, such as spaghettini, linguine or tagliatelle.

1 Cook the pasta in a pan of lightly salted boiling water for 10–12 minutes, until tender, then drain well and return to the pan.

2 Pour the olive oil and lemon juice over the cooked pasta, sprinkle in the slivers of garlic and add seasoning to taste. Toss the pasta over a medium to high heat for 1–2 minutes. Serve immediately in four warmed bowls.

Energy 448kcal/1886kJ; Protein 10.5g; Carbohydrate 64.9g, of which sugars 3g; Fat 18.1g, of which saturates 2.5g; Cholesterol 0mg; Calcium 22mg; Fibre 2.6g; Sodium 3mg

LINGUINE WITH ROCKET

THIS FASHIONABLE LUNCH IS VERY QUICK AND EASY TO MAKE AT HOME. ROCKET HAS AN EXCELLENT PEPPERY FLAVOUR WHICH COMBINES BEAUTIFULLY WITH THE PARMESAN.

Preparation: 3–5 minutes; Cooking: 11–14 minutes

SERVES FOUR

INGREDIENTS

350g/12oz dried linguine
120ml/4fl oz/½ cup extra virgin
  olive oil
1 large bunch rocket (arugula), about
  150g/5oz, stalks removed, shredded
75g/3oz/1 cup freshly grated
  Parmesan cheese

1 Cook the pasta in a large pan of lightly salted boiling water for 10–12 minutes, until tender, then drain thoroughly.

2 Heat about 60ml/4 tbsp of the olive oil in the pasta pan, then add the drained pasta and rocket. Toss over a medium heat for 1–2 minutes, or until the rocket is just wilted, then remove the pan from the heat.

3 Transfer the pasta and rocket to a large, warmed bowl. Add half the freshly grated Parmesan and the remaining olive oil. Add a little salt and black pepper to taste.

4 Toss the mixture quickly to mix all the flavours together and ensure the pasta is well coated with the oil. Serve immediately, sprinkled with the remaining Parmesan.

COOK'S TIPS
• Fresh Parmesan keeps well in the refrigerator for up to a month, if wrapped in greaseproof paper.
• Linguine is an egg pasta and looks rather like flattened strands of spaghetti. Spaghetti, fettucine or pappardelle could be used instead. Dried pasta cooks in just over 10 minutes, but an even faster result can be obtained by using fresh pasta.

Simply add it to a large pan of boiling, lightly salted water, making sure that all the strands are fully submerged, and cook for 2–3 minutes. The pasta is ready when it rises to the top of the pan and has a slight firmness in the centre.

Energy 573kcal/2404kJ; Protein 19g; Carbohydrate 65.4g, of which sugars 3.5g; Fat 28g, of which saturates 6.9g; Cholesterol 19mg; Calcium 311mg; Fibre 3.3g; Sodium 260mg

PASTA WITH FRESH PESTO

BOTTLED PESTO IS A USEFUL INGREDIENT, BUT YOU CAN MAKE YOUR OWN IN LESS TIME THAN IT TAKES TO BOIL THE PASTA THAT ACCOMPANIES IT. ANY SPARE PESTO WILL KEEP FOR A FEW DAYS.

Preparation: 4 minutes; Cooking: 12–14 minutes

SERVES FOUR

INGREDIENTS

400g/14oz/3½ cups dried pasta
50g/2oz/1⅓ cups fresh basil leaves,
    plus extra, to garnish
2–4 garlic cloves
60ml/4 tbsp pine nuts
120ml/4fl oz/½ cup extra virgin
    olive oil
115g/4oz/1⅓ cups freshly grated
    Parmesan cheese, plus extra
    to serve
25g/1oz/⅓ cup freshly grated
    Pecorino cheese
salt and ground black pepper

1 Bring a large pan of lightly salted water to the boil. Add the pasta and cook for 12–14 minutes or according to the instructions on the packet, until just tender but still firm to the bite.

2 Meanwhile, put the basil leaves, garlic and pine nuts in a blender or food processor. Add 60ml/4 tbsp of the olive oil. Process until the ingredients are finely chopped, scraping down the sides of the bowl twice.

3 With the motor running, slowly pour the remaining oil in a thin, steady stream through the feeder tube.

4 Scrape the mixture into a large bowl and beat in the cheeses with a wooden spoon. Taste and add salt and pepper if necessary.

5 Drain the pasta well, then add it to the bowl of pesto and toss to coat. Serve immediately, garnished with the fresh basil leaves. Hand shaved Parmesan around separately.

Energy 783kcal/3279kJ; Protein 27.9g; Carbohydrate 74.7g, of which sugars 3.9g; Fat 43.5g, of which saturates 10.9g; Cholesterol 35mg; Calcium 447mg; Fibre 3.2g; Sodium 385mg

CREAMY LEEK CASSEROLE

Energy 322kcal/1330kJ; Protein 7.8g; Carbohydrate 5g, of which sugars 4g; Fat 29.8g, of which saturates 17.1g; Cholesterol 70mg; Calcium 193mg; Fibre 3.3g; Sodium 147mg

THIS IS QUITE A RICH ACCOMPANIMENT THAT COULD EASILY BE SERVED AS A MEAL IN ITSELF WITH BROWN RICE OR COUSCOUS. FOR A VERY QUICK SNACK, JUST SERVE IT ON TOAST.

Preparation: 3–4 minutes; Cooking: 12 minutes

SERVES FOUR

INGREDIENTS

4 large leeks or 12 baby leeks,
 trimmed and washed
15ml/1 tbsp olive oil
150ml/¼ pint/⅔ cup double
 (heavy) cream
75g/3oz mature (sharp) Cheddar or
 Monterey Jack cheese, grated
salt and ground black pepper

1 If using large leeks, slice them lengthways. Heat the oil in a large frying pan and add the leeks. Season with salt and pepper and cook for about 4 minutes, stirring occasionally, until they become aromatic and the outsides start to turn golden.

2 Preheat the grill (broiler) to high. Pour the cream into the pan, drizzling it over the leeks, and stir until well combined. Lower the heat and allow to bubble gently for a few minutes, but do not over-boil as the cream may begin to curdle.

3 Transfer the creamy leeks to a shallow ovenproof dish and sprinkle with the cheese. Grill (broil) for 4–5 minutes, or until the cheese topping is golden brown and bubbling. Serve immediately.

VARIATIONS

• This recipe works well with all sorts of hard cheeses, from Parmesan and Gran Padano to Red Leicester, Double Gloucester and Caerphilly. Experiment with different flavours to suit your own tastes.

• For a more substantial dish, cook sliced button (white) mushroom with the leeks, or top the mixture with sliced cherry tomatoes before adding the cheese.

• To make the dish more appealing to meat lovers, add some diced smoky bacon or pancetta to the pan in step 1, after you have fried the leeks for a couple of minutes.

WARM PENNE WITH FRESH TOMATOES AND BASIL

WHEN YOU'RE HEADING OFF FOR A FAMILY BIKE RIDE OR A WALK ON THE BEACH, SOMETHING LIGHT AND FRESH, BUT WHICH KEEPS ENERGY LEVELS TOPPED UP OVER TIME, IS JUST WHAT YOU NEED.

Preparation: 2–3 minutes; Cooking: 12–14 minutes

SERVES FOUR

INGREDIENTS
500g/1¼lb dried penne
5 very ripe plum tomatoes
1 small bunch fresh basil
60ml/4 tbsp extra virgin olive oil
salt and ground black pepper

COOK'S TIP
If you cannot find ripe tomatoes, roast those you have to bring out their flavour. Put the tomatoes in a roasting pan, drizzle with oil and roast at 190°C/375°F/Gas 5 for 20 minutes, then mash roughly.

1 Cook the pasta in a large pan of lightly salted boiling water for 12–14 minutes, until tender. Meanwhile, roughly chop the tomatoes and tear up the basil leaves.

2 Drain the pasta thoroughly and return it to the clean pan. Toss with the tomatoes, basil and olive oil. Season with salt and freshly ground black pepper and serve immediately.

Energy 552kcal/2336kJ; Protein 16.3g; Carbohydrate 96.9g, of which sugars 8.3g; Fat 13.8g, of which saturates 2g; Cholesterol 0mg; Calcium 65mg; Fibre 5.5g; Sodium 19mg

EGGS NOODLES <u>WITH</u> PARSLEY AND OLIVES

THIS DISH OF COLD NOODLES MAKES A DELICIOUS MEAL FOR ANY DAY OF THE WEEK. CHILL FOR AS LONG AS POSSIBLE, PREFERABLY OVERNIGHT, TO ALLOW THE FLAVOURS TO DEVELOP.

Preparation: 5 minutes; Cooking: 3–5 minutes; Chilling: 4–8 hours

SERVES FOUR

INGREDIENTS
    250g/9oz dried egg noodles
    30–60ml/2–4 tbsp extra virgin
      olive oil
    3 garlic cloves, finely chopped
    60–90ml/4–6 tbsp/¼–⅓ cup
      coarsely chopped fresh parsley
    25–30 pitted green olives, sliced or
      coarsely chopped
    salt

COOK'S TIP
Use pitted olives for speed. They chop
easily and look great in this dish.

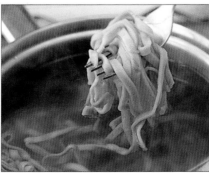

1 Cook the noodles in lightly salted
boiling water as directed on the packet,
or until just tender. Drain and rinse
under cold running water.

2 Tip the noodles into a bowl, then add
the olive oil, garlic, parsley and olives
and toss together to combine well. Chill
before serving.

Energy 352kcal/1476kJ; Protein 8.6g; Carbohydrate 45.3g, of which sugars 1.6g; Fat 16.4g, of which saturates 3.1g; Cholesterol 19mg; Calcium 86mg; Fibre 4.2g; Sodium 1244mg.

MEXICAN TOMATO RICE

VERSIONS OF THIS DISH — A RELATIVE OF SPANISH RICE — ARE POPULAR ALL OVER SOUTH AMERICA.
IT IS A DELICIOUS MEDLEY OF RICE, TOMATOES, PEAS AND AROMATIC FLAVOURINGS.

Preparation: 3 minutes; Cooking: 17 minutes

SERVES FOUR

INGREDIENTS

  400g/14oz can chopped tomatoes in
    tomato juice
  30ml/2 tbsp vegetable oil, preferably
    olive oil
  ½ onion, roughly chopped
  2 garlic cloves, roughly chopped
  500g/1¼lb/2½ cups long grain rice
  750ml/1¼ pints/3 cups
    vegetable stock
  2.5ml/½ tsp salt
  3 fresh chillies
  150g/5oz/1 cup frozen peas
  ground black pepper

COOK'S TIP
The rice makes a good filling for red or
orange (bell) peppers, which have been
halved, seeded and steamed for about
15 minutes, until tender.

1 Pour the tomatoes and juice into a
food processor or blender, and process
until smooth.

2 Heat the oil in a large, heavy pan,
add the onion and garlic and cook over
a medium heat for 2 minutes until
softened. Stir in the rice and stir-fry for
1–2 minutes.

3 Add the tomato mixture and stir over
a medium heat for 3–4 minutes until all
the liquid has been absorbed.

4 Stir in the stock, salt, whole chillies
and peas. Bring to the boil. Cover and
simmer for about 6 minutes, stirring
occasionally, until the rice is just tender.

5 Remove the pan from the heat, cover
it with a tight-fitting lid and leave it to
stand in a warm place for 5 minutes.

6 Remove the chillies, fluff up the rice
lightly with a fork, and serve in warmed
bowls, sprinkled with black pepper.
The chillies can be used as a garnish,
if you like.

Energy 552kcal/2305kJ; Protein 12.7g; Carbohydrate 108.3g, of which sugars 4.8g; Fat 7g, of which saturates 1g; Cholesterol 0mg; Calcium 43mg; Fibre 3g; Sodium 10mg.

COUSCOUS WITH HALLOUMI

VERY OFTEN COUSCOUS IS CONSIDERED A SIDE DISH. HERE, IT PLAYS A LEADING ROLE AND IS TOPPED WITH GRIDDLED SLICED COURGETTES AND HALLOUMI, A MILD CHEESE FROM CYPRUS.

Preparation: 5 minutes; Cooking: 10–12 minutes

SERVES FOUR

INGREDIENTS

30ml/2 tbsp olive oil, plus extra
  for brushing
1 large red onion, chopped
2 garlic cloves, chopped
5ml/1 tsp mild chilli powder
5ml/1 tsp ground cumin
5ml/1 tsp ground coriander
5 cardamom pods, bruised
3 courgettes (zucchini), sliced
  lengthways into ribbons
225g/8oz halloumi cheese, sliced
1 bay leaf
1 cinnamon stick
275g/10oz/1⅔ cups couscous
50g/2oz/¼ cup whole shelled
  almonds, toasted
1 peach, stoned (pitted) and diced
25g/1oz/2 tbsp butter
salt and ground black pepper
chopped fresh flat leaf parsley,
  to garnish

1 Heat the oil in a large heavy pan, add the onion and garlic and sauté for 3–4 minutes until the onion has softened, stirring occasionally.

2 Stir in the chilli powder, cumin, coriander and cardamom pods, and leave the pan over a low heat to allow the flavours to mingle.

3 Meanwhile, brush the courgettes lightly with oil and cook them on a hot griddle or under a hot grill (broiler) for 2–3 minutes, until tender and slightly charred.

4 Turn the courgettes over, add the halloumi and continue cooking for a further 3 minutes, turning the halloumi over once.

5 While the vegetables are cooking, pour 300ml/½ pint/1¼ cups water into a large pan and add the bay leaf and cinnamon stick. Bring to the boil, remove from the heat and immediately add the couscous. Cover and allow to swell for 2 minutes.

6 Add the couscous to the spicy onion mixture, with the almonds, diced peach and butter. Toss over the heat for 2 minutes, then remove the whole spices, arrange the couscous on a plate and season well. Top with the halloumi and courgettes. Sprinkle the parsley over the top and serve.

COOK'S TIP
Look out for packets of flavoured instant couscous at the supermarket. They are very quick and easy to cook, come in a range of flavours and taste delicious. A spiced version would work well in this recipe.

Energy 515kcal/2138kJ; Protein 19.9g; Carbohydrate 42.7g, of which sugars 6.1g; Fat 30.3g, of which saturates 12.5g; Cholesterol 46mg; Calcium 290mg; Fibre 2.9g; Sodium 264mg

SPICED VEGETABLE COUSCOUS

THIS TASTY VEGETARIAN MAIN COURSE IS EASY TO MAKE AND CAN BE PREPARED WITH ANY NUMBER OF YOUNG SEASONAL VEGETABLES SUCH AS SPINACH, LEEKS, PEAS OR CORN.

Preparation: 5 minutes; Cooking: 15 minutes

SERVES SIX

INGREDIENTS

45ml/3 tbsp olive oil
1 large onion, finely chopped
2 garlic cloves, crushed
15ml/1 tbsp tomato purée (paste)
2.5ml/½ tsp ground turmeric
2.5ml/½ tsp cayenne pepper
5ml/1 tsp ground coriander
5ml/1 tsp ground cumin
225g/8oz/1½ cups cauliflower florets
225g/8oz baby carrots, trimmed
1 red (bell) pepper, seeded and diced
225g/8oz courgettes (zucchini), sliced
400g/14oz can chickpeas, drained
   and rinsed
4 beefsteak tomatoes, peeled
   and sliced
45ml/3 tbsp chopped fresh coriander
   (cilantro)
sea salt and ground black pepper
coriander sprigs, to garnish
For the couscous
2.5ml/½ tsp salt
450g/1lb/2⅔ cups couscous
50g/2oz/¼ cup butter

1 Heat 30ml/2 tbsp oil in a large pan, add the onion and garlic and cook until soft and translucent. Stir in the tomato purée, turmeric, cayenne, coriander and cumin. Cook, stirring, for 2 minutes.

2 Add the cauliflower, baby carrots and pepper, with enough water to come halfway up the vegetables. Bring to the boil and cook for 5 minutes.

3 Add the courgettes, chickpeas and tomatoes and cook for 5 minutes. Stir in the fresh coriander and season. Lower the heat to a bare simmer.

4 Cook the couscous. Bring about 475ml/16fl oz/2 cups water to the boil in a large pan. Add the remaining olive oil and the salt. Remove from the heat and add the couscous, stirring. Allow to swell for 2 minutes.

5 Add the butter, and heat through gently, stirring to separate the grains.

6 Turn the couscous out on to a warm serving dish and place the cooked vegetables on top, pouring over any liquid. Garnish with coriander sprigs and serve immediately.

Energy 419kcal/1749kJ; Protein 12.9g; Carbohydrate 61.8g, of which sugars 11.8g; Fat 14.8g, of which saturates 1.9g; Cholesterol 0mg; Calcium 87mg; Fibre 6.7g; Sodium 178mg

MUSHROOM STROGANOFF

THIS CREAMY MIXED MUSHROOM SAUCE TASTES GREAT AND IS IDEAL FOR A DINNER PARTY.
SERVE IT WITH TOASTED BUCKWHEAT, BROWN RICE OR A MIXTURE OF WILD RICES.

Preparation: 3 minutes; Cooking: 15–17 minutes

SERVES FOUR

INGREDIENTS
   25g/1oz/2 tbsp butter
   900g/2lb/8 cups mixed mushrooms,
      cut into bite-size pieces
   350g/12oz/1¾ cups white long
      grain rice
   350ml/12fl oz/1½ cups white
      wine sauce
   250ml/8fl oz/1 cup sour cream
   chopped chives, to garnish

1 Melt the butter in a large, heavy pan and add the mushrooms. Cook over a medium heat until the mushrooms give up their liquid. Continue cooking until they are tender and beginning to brown.

2 Meanwhile, bring a large pan of lightly salted water to the boil. Add the rice, partially cover the pan and cook over a medium heat for 13–15 minutes until the rice is just tender.

3 Add the wine sauce to the cooked mushrooms in the pan and bring to the boil, stirring. Stir in the sour cream and season to taste. Drain the rice well, spoon on to warm plates, top with the sauce and garnish with chives.

Energy 556kcal/2316kJ; Protein 13.3g; Carbohydrate 80.4g, of which sugars 7.2g; Fat 21.7g, of which saturates 11.4g; Cholesterol 51mg; Calcium 96mg; Fibre 2.5g; Sodium 897mg

PASTA WITH SUN-DRIED TOMATOES

THIS IS A LIGHT, MODERN PASTA DISH OF THE KIND SERVED IN FASHIONABLE RESTAURANTS.
IT IS NOT ONLY QUICK AND EASY TO PREPARE, IT LOOKS STUNNING TOO.
Preparation: 3 minutes; Cooking: 13–15 minutes

SERVES FOUR TO SIX

INGREDIENTS
  45ml/3 tbsp pine nuts
  350g/12oz dried paglia e fieno (or
    two different colours of tagliatelle)
  45ml/3 tbsp extra virgin olive oil or
    sunflower oil
  30ml/2 tbsp sun-dried tomato
    purée (paste)
  2 pieces drained sun-dried tomatoes
    in olive oil, cut into very thin slivers
  40g/1½oz radicchio leaves,
    finely shredded
  4–6 spring onions (scallions), thinly
    sliced into rings
  salt and ground black pepper

1 Put the pine nuts in a non-stick frying pan and toss over a low to medium heat for 1–2 minutes or until they are lightly toasted and golden. Remove from the pan and set aside.

2 Cook the pasta in lightly salted water for 12–14 minutes or until tender, keeping the colours separate by using two pans.

3 While the pasta is cooking, heat 15ml/1 tbsp of the oil in a medium pan or frying pan. Add the sun-dried tomato paste and the sun-dried tomatoes, then stir in 2 ladlefuls of the water used for cooking the pasta. Simmer until the sauce is slightly reduced, stirring constantly.

4 Mix in the shredded radicchio, then taste and season if necessary. Keep on a low heat. Drain the paglia e fieno, keeping the colours separate, and return the pasta to the pans. Add about 15ml/1 tbsp oil to each pan and toss over a medium to high heat until the pasta is glistening with the oil.

5 Arrange a portion of green and white pasta in each of 4–6 warmed bowls, then spoon the sun-dried tomato and radicchio mixture in the centre. Sprinkle the spring onions and pine nuts over the top and serve immediately. Before eating, each diner should toss the sauce ingredients with the pasta.

COOK'S TIP
If you find the presentation too fussy, you can toss the tomato and raddichio mixture with the pasta in a large bowl before serving, then sprinkle the spring onions and toasted pine nuts on top.

Energy 309kcal/1302kJ; Protein 8.6g; Carbohydrate 44.9g, of which sugars 3.6g; Fat 11.8g, of which saturates 1.3g; Cholesterol 0mg; Calcium 23mg; Fibre 2.3g; Sodium 16mg

GARGANELLI PASTA WITH ASPARAGUS AND CREAM

WHEN FRESH ASPARAGUS IS ON SALE AT THE MARKET, THIS IS A WONDERFUL WAY TO SERVE IT. ANY TYPE OF PASTA CAN BE USED, BUT ONE THAT MIRRORS THE SHAPE OF THE ASPARAGUS WORKS BEST.

Preparation: 4–5 minutes; Cooking: 15 minutes

SERVES FOUR

INGREDIENTS

1 bunch fresh young asparagus,
  250–300g/9–11oz
350g/12oz/3 cups dried garganelli
25g/1oz/2 tbsp butter
200ml/7fl oz/scant 1 cup panna da
  cucina or double (heavy) cream
30ml/2 tbsp dry white wine
90–115g/3½–4oz/1–1⅓ cups freshly
  grated Parmesan cheese
30ml/2 tbsp chopped fresh mixed
  herbs, such as basil, flat leaf
  parsley, chervil, marjoram
  and oregano
salt and ground black pepper

1 Snap off and throw away the woody ends of the asparagus – after trimming, you should have about 200g/7oz asparagus spears. Cut the spears diagonally into pieces about the same length and shape as the garganelli.

2 Blanch the thicker asparagus pieces in a large pan of lightly salted boiling water for 2 minutes, the tips for 1 minute. Using a slotted spoon, transfer the blanched asparagus to a colander, rinse under cold water and set aside.

3 Bring the water in the pan back to the boil, add the pasta and cook for 12 minutes or until tender.

4 Meanwhile, melt the butter in a heavy pan. Add the cream, with salt and pepper to taste, and bring to the boil. Simmer for a few minutes until the cream reduces and thickens.

5 Stir the asparagus, wine and about half the Parmesan into the sauce. Drain the pasta and return it to the clean pan. Add the sauce and herbs and toss. Serve with the remaining Parmesan.

Energy 716kcal/2994kJ; Protein 22g; Carbohydrate 67g, of which sugars 5g; Fat 41.3g, of which saturates 24.8g; Cholesterol 104mg; Calcium 335mg; Fibre 3.6g; Sodium 298mg

SOUFFLÉ OMELETTE <u>WITH</u> MUSHROOMS

A SOUFFLÉ OMELETTE MAKES AN IDEAL MEAL FOR ONE, ESPECIALLY WITH THIS DELICIOUS FILLING,
BUT BE WARNED — WHEN OTHERS SMELL IT COOKING THEY ARE LIKELY TO DEMAND THEIR SHARE.

Preparation: 5 minutes; Cooking: 13–15 minutes

SERVES ONE

INGREDIENTS
   2 eggs, separated
   15g/½oz/1 tbsp butter
   flat leaf parsley or coriander
     (cilantro) leaves, to garnish
For the mushroom sauce
   15g/½oz/1 tbsp butter
   75g/3oz/generous 1 cup button
     (white) mushrooms, thinly sliced
   15ml/1 tbsp plain (all-purpose) flour
   85–120ml/3–4fl oz/⅓–½ cup milk
   5ml/1 tsp chopped fresh parsley
   salt and ground black pepper

COOK'S TIP
For extra flavour, add a few drops of soy
sauce to the mushrooms.

1 To make the mushroom sauce, melt
the butter in a pan or frying pan and
add the sliced mushrooms. Fry gently
for 4–5 minutes, stirring occasionally.
The mushrooms will exude quite a
lot of liquid, but this will rapidly
be reabsorbed.

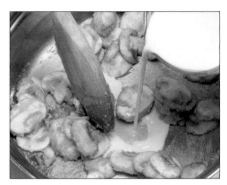

2 Stir in the flour, then gradually add
the milk, stirring all the time. Cook
until the sauce boils and thickens. Add
the parsley, if using, and season with
salt and pepper. Keep warm.

3 Make the omelette. Beat the egg yolks
with 15ml/1 tbsp water and season with
a little salt and pepper. Whisk the egg
whites until stiff, then fold into the egg
yolks. Preheat the grill (broiler).

4 Melt the butter in a large frying pan
and pour in the egg mixture. Cook over
a gentle heat for 2–4 minutes. Place the
frying pan under the grill and cook for
a further 3–4 minutes until the top is
golden brown.

5 Slide the omelette on to a warmed
serving plate, pour the mushroom sauce
over the top and fold the omelette in
half. Serve, garnished with parsley.

Energy 838kcal/3514kJ; Protein 45.5g; Carbohydrate 53.7g, of which sugars 42.1g; Fat 51.4g, of which saturates 28.3g; Cholesterol 497mg; Calcium 1150mg; Fibre 1.3g; Sodium 707mg

SPICY OMELETTE

THE ACCUSATION THAT EGG DISHES CAN BE A BIT BLAND COULD NEVER BE LEVELLED AT THIS SPICY, VEGETABLE-RICH DISH. IT COMES FROM INDIA, WHERE IT IS OFTEN SERVED FOR BREAKFAST.

Preparation: 6–7 minutes; Cooking: 10 minutes

SERVES FOUR TO SIX

INGREDIENTS

30ml/2 tbsp vegetable oil
1 onion, finely chopped
2.5ml/½ tsp ground cumin
1 garlic clove, crushed
1 or 2 fresh green chillies,
    finely chopped
a few coriander (cilantro) sprigs,
    chopped, plus extra, to garnish
1 firm tomato, chopped
1 small potato, cubed and boiled
25g/1oz/¼ cup cooked peas
25g/1oz/¼ cup cooked corn,
    or drained canned corn
2 eggs, beaten
25g/1oz/¼ cup grated cheese
salt and ground black pepper

1 Heat the vegetable oil in a wok, karahi or large pan, and fry the next nine ingredients for 2–3 minutes until they are well blended but the potato and tomato are still firm. Season with salt and ground black pepper.

2 Increase the heat and pour in the beaten eggs. Reduce the heat, cover and cook until the bottom of the omelette is golden brown. Sprinkle the omelette with the grated cheese. Place under a hot grill (broiler) and cook until the egg sets and the cheese has melted.

3 Garnish the omelette with sprigs of coriander and serve with salad for a light lunch or supper.

VARIATION
You can use any vegetable with the potatoes. Try adding thickly sliced mushrooms instead of the corn.

Energy 93kcal/388kJ; Protein 4g; Carbohydrate 3.7g, of which sugars 1.2g; Fat 7.1g, of which saturates 1.9g; Cholesterol 67mg; Calcium 46mg; Fibre 0.6g; Sodium 104mg

TOFU AND PEPPER KEBABS

A SIMPLE COATING OF GROUND, DRY-ROASTED PEANUTS PRESSED ON TO CUBED TOFU PROVIDES PLENTY OF ADDITIONAL FLAVOUR ALONG WITH THE PEPPERS. USE METAL OR BAMBOO SKEWERS.

Preparation: 6–8 minutes; Cooking: 10–12 minutes

SERVES FOUR

INGREDIENTS
250g/9oz firm tofu
50g/2oz/½ cup dry-roasted peanuts
2 red and 2 green (bell) peppers
60ml/4 tbsp sweet chilli
dipping sauce

1 Pat the tofu dry on kitchen paper and then cut it into small cubes. Grind the peanuts in a blender or food processor and transfer to a plate.

COOK'S TIP
Don't forget to soak the bamboo skewers upright in a jar of water for about half an hour before using, so they don't scorch.

2 Preheat the grill (broiler) to medium. Using a sharp knife, halve and seed the red and green peppers, and cut them into large chunks. Turn the tofu cubes in the ground nuts to coat thoroughly on all sides.

3 Thread the chunks of pepper on to four large skewers with the tofu cubes and place on a foil-lined grill rack. Grill (broil) the kebabs, turning frequently, for 10–12 minutes, or until the peppers and peanuts are beginning to brown.

Energy 175kcal/730kJ; Protein 10g; Carbohydrate 12.9g, of which sugars 11.4g; Fat 9.6g, of which saturates 1.6g; Cholesterol 0mg; Calcium 339mg; Fibre 3.6g; Sodium 108mg

STUFFED SWEET PEPPERS

THIS IS AN UNUSUAL RECIPE IN THAT THE STUFFED PEPPERS ARE STEAMED RATHER THAN BAKED. THE TECHNIQUE IS SPEEDY AND THE RESULT IS BEAUTIFULLY LIGHT AND TENDER.

Preparation: 5 minutes; Cooking: 15 minutes

SERVES FOUR

INGREDIENTS
3 garlic cloves, finely chopped
2 coriander (cilantro) roots,
  finely chopped
400g/14oz/3 cups
  mushrooms, quartered
5ml/1 tsp Thai red curry paste
1 egg, lightly beaten
15–30ml/1–2 tbsp light soy sauce
2.5ml/½ tsp granulated sugar
3 kaffir lime leaves, finely chopped
4 yellow (bell) peppers, halved
  lengthways and seeded

VARIATIONS
Use red or orange (bell) peppers if you
prefer, or a combination of the two.

1 In a mortar or spice grinder pound or blend the garlic with the coriander roots. Scrape into a bowl.

2 Put the mushrooms in a food processor and pulse briefly until they are finely chopped. Add to the garlic mixture, then stir in the curry paste, egg, sauces, sugar and lime leaves.

3 Place the pepper halves in a single layer in a steamer basket. Spoon the mixture loosely into the pepper halves.

4 Bring the water in the steamer to the boil, then lower the heat to a simmer. Steam the peppers for 15 minutes, or until the flesh feels tender when tested with a knife tip. Serve hot.

Energy 89kcal/374kJ; Protein 5.1g; Carbohydrate 10.6g, of which sugars 9.9g; Fat 3.2g, of which saturates 0.8g; Cholesterol 48mg; Calcium 27mg; Fibre 3.5g; Sodium 563mg

FIORENTINA PIZZA

AN EGG ADDS THE FINISHING TOUCH TO THIS CLASSIC ITALIAN SPINACH PIZZA; TRY NOT TO OVERCOOK IT THOUGH, AS IT'S BEST WHEN THE YOLK IS STILL SLIGHTLY SOFT IN THE MIDDLE.

Preparation: 2 minutes; Cooking: 18 minutes

SERVES TWO TO THREE

INGREDIENTS

45ml/3 tbsp olive oil
1 small red onion, thinly sliced
175g/6oz fresh spinach,
  stalks removed
1 pizza base, about 25–30cm/
  10–12in in diameter
1 small jar pizza sauce
freshly grated nutmeg
150g/5oz mozzarella cheese
1 egg
25g/1oz/¼ cup Gruyère
  cheese, grated

1 Heat 15ml/1 tbsp of the oil and fry the onion until soft. Add the spinach and fry until wilted. Drain any excess liquid.

2 Preheat the oven to 220°C/425°F/ Gas 7. Brush the pizza base with half the remaining olive oil. Spread the pizza sauce evenly over the base, using the back of a spoon, then top with the spinach mixture. Sprinkle over a little freshly grated nutmeg.

3 Thinly slice the mozzarella and arrange over the spinach. Drizzle over the remaining oil. Bake for 10 minutes, then remove from the oven.

4 Make a small well in the centre of the pizza topping and carefully break the egg into the hole. Sprinkle over the grated Gruyère cheese and return the pizza to the oven for a further 5–10 minutes until crisp and golden. Serve immediately.

VARIATION
A calzone is like a pizza but is folded in half to conceal the filling. Add the egg with the rest of the pizza topping, fold over the dough, seal the edges and bake for 20 minutes.

Energy 503kcal/2100kJ; Protein 20.8g; Carbohydrate 40.3g, of which sugars 5.9g; Fat 29.7g, of which saturates 10.9g; Cholesterol 101mg; Calcium 417mg; Fibre 2.8g; Sodium 668mg.

FOUR CHEESE CIABATTA PIZZA

FEW DISHES ARE AS SIMPLE — OR AS SATISFYING — AS THIS PIZZA MADE BY TOPPING A HALVED LOAF OF CIABATTA. THIS IS THE SORT OF THING CHILDREN COULD MAKE TO GIVE MUM AND DAD A BREAK.

Preparation: 4 minutes; Cooking: 10–12 minutes

SERVES TWO

INGREDIENTS

1 loaf ciabatta bread
1 garlic clove, halved
30–45ml/2–3 tbsp olive oil
about 90ml/6 tbsp passata (bottled
 strained tomatoes) or sugocasa
1 small red onion, thinly sliced
30ml/2 tbsp chopped pitted olives
about 50g/2oz each of four cheeses,
 one mature/sharp (Parmesan or
 Cheddar), one blue-veined
 (Gorgonzola or Stilton), one mild
 (Fontina or Emmental) and a goat's
 cheese, sliced, grated or crumbled
pine nuts or cumin seeds, to sprinkle
salt and ground black pepper
sprigs of basil, to garnish

1 Preheat the oven to 200°C/400°F/ Gas 6. Split the ciabatta bread in half. Rub the cut sides with the garlic, then brush over the oil. Spread with the passata or sugocasa, then add the onion slices and olives. Season to taste with salt and black pepper.

2 Divide the cheeses between the ciabatta halves and sprinkle over the pine nuts or cumin seeds. Bake for 10–12 minutes, until bubbling and golden brown. Cut the pizza into slices and serve immediately, garnished with the sprigs of fresh basil.

Energy 782kcal/3265kJ; Protein 34g; Carbohydrate 55.8g, of which sugars 6.2g; Fat 47.4g, of which saturates 22.8g; Cholesterol 86mg; Calcium 756mg; Fibre 3.4g; Sodium 1952mg

SWEET PEPPERS STUFFED WITH TWO CHEESES

A DELICIOUS BARBECUE STARTER TO COOK BEFORE THE GRILL TASTES TOO STRONGLY OF MEAT.
ALTERNATIVELY, USE A DISPOSABLE BARBECUE FOR THESE TASTY PEPPERS.

Preparation: 5 minutes; Cooking: 12–14 minutes

SERVES FOUR

INGREDIENTS

    4 sweet romano peppers, preferably
      in mixed colours, total weight about
      350g/12oz
    90ml/6 tbsp extra virgin olive oil
    200g/7oz mozzarella cheese
    10 drained bottled sweet cherry
      peppers, finely chopped
    115g/4oz ricotta salata
    30ml/2 tbsp chopped fresh
      oregano leaves
    24 black olives
    2 garlic cloves, crushed
    salt and ground black pepper
    dressed mixed salad leaves and
      bread, to serve

1 Prepare a barbecue. Split the peppers lengthways and remove the seeds and membrane. Rub 15ml/1 tbsp of the oil all over the peppers. Place them hollow-side uppermost.

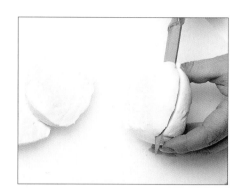

2 Slice the mozzarella and divide it equally among the pepper halves.

3 Sprinkle over the chopped cherry peppers, season lightly and crumble the ricotta salata over the top, followed by the oregano leaves and olives.

4 Mix the garlic with the remaining oil, add a little salt and pepper, and whisk to combine. Spoon about half the mixture over the filling in the peppers.

5 Once the flames have died down, rake the coals to one side. Position a lightly oiled grill rack over the coals to heat. When the coals are medium-hot, or with a moderate coating of ash, place the filled peppers on the section of grill rack that is not over the coals.

6 Cover with a lid, or improvise with a wok lid or tented heavy-duty foil. Grill for 6 minutes, then spoon the remaining oil mixture over the filling, replace the lid and continue to grill for 6–8 minutes more, or until the peppers are lightly charred and the cheese has melted. Serve with a dressed green or leafy salad and bread.

VARIATION
The peppers can be cooked on a griddle if you prefer. It is a good idea to blanch them in boiling water before filling, to give them a head start.

Energy 371kcal/1532kJ; Protein 13.1g; Carbohydrate 6.6g, of which sugars 6.3g; Fat 32.6g, of which saturates 12.2g; Cholesterol 41mg; Calcium 203mg; Fibre 2g; Sodium 484mg

SUMMER VEGETABLE KEBABS WITH HARISSA

EATING IN THE GARDEN IS ONE OF THE PLEASURES OF SUMMER. THIS WOULD BE LOVELY FOR LUNCH OR AS AN APPETIZER FOR GUESTS TO NIBBLE WHILE WAITING FOR MORE FILLING BARBECUE FARE.

Preparation: 7 minutes; Cooking: 8–10 minutes

SERVES FOUR

INGREDIENTS
60ml/4 tbsp olive oil
juice of ½ lemon
1 garlic clove, crushed
5ml/1 tsp ground coriander
5ml/1 tsp ground cinnamon
10ml/2 tsp clear honey
2 aubergines (eggplants), part peeled
    and cut into chunks
2 courgettes (zucchini), cut
    into chunks
2–3 red or green (bell) peppers,
    seeded and cut into chunks
12–16 cherry tomatoes
4 small red onions, quartered
5ml/1 tsp salt
For the harissa and yogurt dip
450g/1lb/2 cups Greek (US strained
    plain) yogurt
30–60ml/2–4 tbsp harissa
a small bunch of fresh coriander
    (cilantro), finely chopped
a small bunch of mint, finely chopped
salt and ground black pepper

1 Preheat the grill (broiler) or prepare a barbecue. Mix the olive oil, lemon juice and garlic in a bowl. Add ground coriander, cinnamon, honey and salt.

2 Add the aubergine and courgette chunks, with the peppers, cherry tomatoes and onion quarters. Stir to mix, then thread a generous number of vegetable pieces on to skewers, so that they are just touching each other.

3 Cook the kebabs under the grill or over the coals, turning occasionally until the vegetables are browned all over.

4 Meanwhile, make the dip. Put the yogurt in a bowl and beat in harissa to taste. Add most of the coriander and mint, reserving a little to garnish, and season well with salt and pepper.

5 As soon as the kebabs are cooked, serve on a bed of couscous and sprinkle with the remaining fresh coriander. Spoon a little of the yogurt dip on the side, and put the rest in a small serving bowl.

COOK'S TIP
As well as being a quick-cook aid, metal skewers enhance presentation tremendously.

Energy 305kcal/1267kJ; Protein 9.9g; Carbohydrate 24.8g, of which sugars 22.6g; Fat 19.1g, of which saturates 6.6g; Cholesterol 16mg; Calcium 230mg; Fibre 5.2g; Sodium 181mg

ON THE SIDE

This selection of vegetable side salads and cooked accompaniments will complement just about every type of main course dish you can think of, and some could even be enjoyed as appetizers. Among the quick yet innovative dishes here is a salad of Warm Halloumi and Fennel, infused with lemon and olive oil — a wonderful summer-style recipe. By contrast, the down-to-earth, Irish-inspired Carrot and Parsnip Purée is a lovely variation on the traditional mashed potato accompaniment, and simply cries out for cold winter evenings and warming stew-style dishes. For the party menu, there are three types of tapas, all of which are best made ahead to allow time for the flavours to develop, while the toffee-like texture of Caramelized Shallots are a delightful, unusual side for that big occasion roast dinner. Two of the spicier offerings here, Spicy Potato and Olive Salad, and Masala Green Beans with Fenugreek, take familiar vegetables and combine them with a subtle blend of spices to create a pair of unique cooked vegetable accompaniments — both can be served on the side of main course dishes, or as part of buffet.

Left: The recipe for Caramelized Shallots uses red wine, port or Madeira with golden caster sugar to achieve the crisp, sweet coating. It is important to cook the shallots over a high heat, so that the liquid really bubbles and eventually evaporates, to attain that glazed texture.

SIMPLE RICE SALAD

*SOMETIMES CALLED CONFETTI SALAD, THIS FEATURES BRIGHTLY COLOURED CHOPPED VEGETABLES
SERVED IN A WELL-FLAVOURED DRESSING. CHILL IT WELL IF YOU INTEND TO TAKE IT ON A PICNIC.*

Preparation: 6 minutes; Cooking: 10–12 minutes

SERVES SIX

INGREDIENTS

  275g/10oz/1½ cups long grain rice
  1 bunch spring onions (scallions),
    finely sliced
  1 green (bell) pepper, seeded and
    finely diced
  1 yellow (bell) pepper, seeded and
    finely diced
  225g/8oz tomatoes, peeled, seeded
    and chopped
  30ml/2 tbsp chopped fresh flat leaf
    parsley or coriander (cilantro)
For the dressing
  75ml/5 tbsp mixed olive oil and extra
    virgin olive oil
  15ml/1 tbsp sherry vinegar
  5ml/1 tsp strong Dijon mustard
  salt and ground black pepper

1 Cook the rice in a large pan of lightly salted boiling water for 10–12 minutes, until tender but still *al dente*. Be careful not to overcook it.

2 Drain the rice well in a sieve (strainer), rinse thoroughly under cold running water and drain again. Leave the rice to cool while you prepare the ingredients for the dressing.

3 Meanwhile, make the dressing by whisking all the ingredients together. Transfer the rice to a bowl and add half the dressing to moisten it and cool it further.

4 Add the spring onions, peppers, tomatoes and parsley or coriander with the remaining dressing, and toss well to mix. Season with salt and pepper to taste.

Energy 276kcal/1150kJ; Protein 4.6g; Carbohydrate 41.9g, of which sugars 5.2g; Fat 9.9g, of which saturates 1.4g; Cholesterol 0mg; Calcium 29mg; Fibre 1.7g; Sodium 8mg

ENSALADILLA

ALSO KNOWN AS RUSSIAN SALAD, THIS MIXTURE OF COOKED AND RAW VEGETABLES IN A RICH GARLIC MAYONNAISE MAKES A USEFUL VEGETARIAN MAIN COURSE. IT TASTES GOOD WITH HARD-BOILED EGGS.

Preparation: 10 minutes; Cooking: 8 minutes

SERVES FOUR

INGREDIENTS

8 new potatoes, scrubbed
  and quartered
1 large carrot, diced
115g/4oz fine green beans,
  cut into 2cm/¾ in lengths
75g/3oz/¾ cup peas
½ Spanish (Bermuda) onion, chopped
4 cornichons or small
  gherkins, sliced
1 small red (bell) pepper, seeded
  and diced
50g/2oz/½ cup pitted black olives
15ml/1 tbsp drained pickled capers
15ml/1 tbsp freshly squeezed
  lemon juice
30ml/2 tbsp chopped fresh fennel
  or parsley
salt and ground black pepper
For the aioli
2–3 garlic cloves, finely chopped
2.5ml/½ tsp salt
150ml/¼ pint/⅔ cup mayonnaise

1 Make the aioli. Put two or three garlic cloves, depending on their size, in a mortar. Add the salt and crush to a paste. Whisk or stir into the mayonnaise.

VARIATION
This salad is delicious using any combination of chopped, cooked vegetables. Use whatever is available.

2 Cook the potatoes and diced carrot in a pan of boiling lightly salted water for 5 minutes, until almost tender.

3 Add the beans and peas to the potatoes and carrot and cook for 2 minutes, or until all the vegetables are tender but the beans still retain some crunch. Drain and transfer to a bowl of iced water to cool quickly.

4 When cool, drain the vegetables, place them in a large bowl and add the onion, cornichons or gherkins, red pepper, olives and capers. Stir in the aioli and pepper and lemon juice to taste.

5 Toss the vegetables and aioli together until well combined, check the seasoning and chill well. Serve garnished with fennel or parsley.

Energy 395kcal/1636kJ; Protein 5.2g; Carbohydrate 25.6g, of which sugars 8.1g; Fat 30.9g, of which saturates 4.8g; Cholesterol 28mg; Calcium 68mg; Fibre 4.9g; Sodium 472mg

TAPAS OF ALMONDS, OLIVES AND CHEESE

SERVING A FEW CHOICE NIBBLES WITH DRINKS IS THE PERFECT WAY TO GET AN EVENING OFF TO A GOOD START, AND WHEN YOU CAN GET EVERYTHING READY AHEAD OF TIME, LIFE'S EASIER ALL ROUND.

Preparation: 10–15 minutes; Cooking: 5 minutes; Make ahead

SERVES SIX TO EIGHT

INGREDIENTS

For the marinated olives
- 2.5ml/½ tsp coriander seeds
- 2.5ml/½ tsp fennel seeds
- 2 garlic cloves, crushed
- 5ml/1 tsp chopped fresh rosemary
- 10ml/2 tsp chopped fresh parsley
- 15ml/1 tbsp sherry vinegar
- 30ml/2 tbsp olive oil
- 115g/4oz/⅔ cup black olives
- 115g/4oz/⅔ cup green olives

For the marinated cheese
- 150g/5oz Manchego or other firm cheese
- 90ml/6 tbsp olive oil
- 15ml/1 tbsp white wine vinegar
- 5ml/1 tsp black peppercorns
- 1 garlic clove, sliced
- fresh thyme or tarragon sprigs
- fresh flat leaf parsley or tarragon sprigs, to garnish (optional)

For the salted almonds
- 1.5ml/¼ tsp cayenne pepper
- 30ml/2 tbsp sea salt
- 25g/1oz/2 tbsp butter
- 60ml/4 tbsp olive oil
- 200g/7oz/1¾ cups blanched almonds
- extra salt for sprinkling (optional)

1 To make the marinated olives, crush the coriander and fennel seeds in a mortar with a pestle. Work in the garlic, then add the rosemary, parsley, vinegar and olive oil. Mix well. Put the olives in a small bowl and pour over the marinade. Cover with clear film (plastic wrap) and chill for up to 1 week.

2 To make the marinated cheese, cut the Manchego or other firm cheese into bitesize pieces, removing any rind, and put in a small bowl. Combine the oil, vinegar, peppercorns, garlic, thyme or tarragon and pour over the cheese. Cover with clear film and chill for up to 3 days.

3 To make the salted almonds, combine the cayenne pepper and salt in a bowl. Melt the butter with the oil in a frying pan. Add the almonds and fry them, stirring, for 5 minutes, or until golden.

4 Tip the almonds into the salt mixture and toss until the almonds are coated. Leave to cool, then store in an airtight container for up to 1 week.

5 To serve, arrange the almonds, olives and cheese in three separate small, shallow dishes. Garnish the cheese with fresh herbs if you like and sprinkle the almonds with a little more salt, to taste. Provide cocktail sticks (toothpicks) so that guests can pick up the cheese and olives easily.

COOK'S TIPS
- Whole olives, sold with the stone, invariably taste better than pitted ones. Don't serve them directly from the brine, but drain and rinse them, then pat dry with kitchen paper. Put the olives in a jar and pour over extra virgin olive oil to cover. Seal and store in the refrigerator for 1–2 months; the flavour of the olives will become richer. Serve the olives as a tapas dish, or add to salads. When the olives have been eaten, the fruity oil can be used as a dressing for hot food, or made into flavoursome salad dressings.
- A number of exotic stuffed olives are exported from Spain and are widely available in most large supermarkets. Popular varieties include pimiento-stuffed olives, which have been in existence for more than half a century; olives stuffed with salted anchovies; and olives filled with roast garlic.

Energy 383kcal/1580kJ; Protein 10.3g; Carbohydrate 1.8g, of which sugars 1.1g; Fat 36.8g, of which saturates 8.9g; Cholesterol 25mg; Calcium 217mg; Fibre 2.7g; Sodium 1051mg

WILTED SPINACH <u>WITH</u> RICE <u>AND</u> DILL

SPINACH AND RICE MAKES A VERY SUCCESSFUL COMBINATION. THIS IS A DELICIOUS DISH THAT CAN BE MADE IN VERY LITTLE TIME. SERVE IT SOLO OR WITH FRIED OR GRILLED FISH.

Preparation: 4 minutes; Cooking: 13 minutes

SERVES FOUR

INGREDIENTS

  675g/1½lb fresh spinach, trimmed
    of any hard stalks
  105ml/7 tbsp extra virgin olive oil
  1 large onion, chopped
  juice of ½ lemon
  150ml/¼ pint/⅔ cup water
  115g/4oz/generous ½ cup
    long grain rice
  45ml/3 tbsp chopped fresh dill,
    plus extra sprigs to garnish
  salt and ground black pepper

1 Thoroughly wash the spinach in several changes of cold water until clean, then drain it in a colander. Shake off the excess water and put the spinach leaves on a board. Shred them coarsely.

2 Heat the olive oil in a large pan and sauté the onion until translucent. Add the spinach and stir for a few minutes to coat it with the oil.

VARIATION
Baby broad (fava) beans go well with the rice and spinach. Add them to the rice for the final 5 minutes or so.

3 As soon as the spinach looks wilted, add the lemon juice and the measured water and bring to the boil. Add the rice and half of the dill, then cover and cook gently for about 10 minutes or until the rice is cooked to your taste.

4 Spoon into a serving dish and sprinkle the sprigs of dill over the top.

Energy 337kcal/1392kJ; Protein 7.5g; Carbohydrate 29.6g, of which sugars 5.3g; Fat 20.8g, of which saturates 2.9g; Cholesterol 0mg; Calcium 305mg; Fibre 4.3g; Sodium 238mg

WARM HALLOUMI AND FENNEL SALAD

HALLOUMI IS A ROBUST CHEESE THAT HOLDS ITS SHAPE WHEN COOKED ON A GRIDDLE OR BARBECUE.
DURING COOKING IT ACQUIRES THE DISTINCTIVE GRIDDLE MARKS THAT LOOK SO EFFECTIVE HERE.

Preparation: 13 minutes; Cooking: 6 minutes

SERVES FOUR

INGREDIENTS
   200g/7oz halloumi cheese,
     thickly sliced
   2 fennel bulbs, trimmed and
     thinly sliced
   30ml/2 tbsp roughly chopped
     fresh oregano
   45ml/3 tbsp lemon-infused olive oil
   salt and ground black pepper

COOK'S TIP
If you have time, chill the halloumi and
fennel mixture for about 2 hours before
cooking, so it becomes infused with
the dressing.

1 Put the halloumi, fennel and oregano
in a bowl and drizzle over the lemon-
infused oil. Season with salt and black
pepper to taste. (Halloumi is a fairly
salty cheese, so be very careful when
adding extra salt.)

2 Cover the bowl with clear film (plastic
wrap) and set aside for 10 minutes.

3 Place the halloumi and fennel on a
hot griddle pan or over the barbecue,
reserving the marinade, and cook
for about 3 minutes on each side,
until charred.

4 Divide the halloumi and fennel among
four serving plates and drizzle over the
reserved marinade. Serve immediately.

Energy 212kcal/876kJ; Protein 10g; Carbohydrate 1.4g, of which sugars 1.3g; Fat 18.6g, of which saturates 8.1g; Cholesterol 29mg; Calcium 199mg; Fibre 1.8g; Sodium 206mg

CARROT AND PARSNIP PURÉE

PURÉED VEGETABLES AREN'T JUST FOR THE UNDER FIVES. THEIR CREAMINESS APPEALS TO ALL AGES, AND THEY ARE IDEAL PARTNERS FOR CRISP VEGETABLES SUCH AS LIGHTLY COOKED GREEN BEANS.

Preparation: 3 minutes; Cooking: 15–17 minutes

SERVES SIX TO EIGHT

INGREDIENTS
   350g/12oz carrots
   450g/1lb parsnips
   a pinch of freshly grated nutmeg
     or ground mace
   15g/½oz/1 tbsp butter
   about 15ml/1 tbsp single (light)
     cream or crème fraîche
   a small bunch of parsley, chopped,
     plus extra to garnish
   salt and ground black pepper

1 Peel the carrots and slice fairly thinly. Peel the parsnips and cut into bitesize chunks (they are softer and will cook more quickly than the carrots).

2 Boil the carrots and parsnips in separate pans of salted water until tender. Drain them well, then purée in a food processor, with the grated nutmeg or mace, a generous seasoning of salt and ground black pepper, and the butter. Whizz until smooth.

3 Transfer the purée to a bowl and beat in the cream or crème fraîche. Add the chopped parsley for extra flavour.

4 Transfer the carrot and parsnip purée to a warmed serving bowl, sprinkle with the remaining chopped parsley to garnish, and serve hot.

COOK'S TIP
• Any leftover purée can be thinned to taste with good quality chicken or vegetable stock and heated to make a quick home-made soup.
• The carrots can be substituted altogether for a small sweet potato. Peel and dice finely. As with the carrots, boil the sweet potato a little ahead of the parsnips if possible.

Energy 71kcal/298kJ; Protein 1.5g; Carbohydrate 10.7g, of which sugars 6.6g; Fat 2.7g, of which saturates 1.4g; Cholesterol 5mg; Calcium 49mg; Fibre 4g; Sodium 31mg

CARAMELIZED SHALLOTS

SWEET, GOLDEN SHALLOTS ARE GOOD WITH ALL SORTS OF MAIN DISHES, INCLUDING POULTRY OR MEAT.
THEY ALSO TASTE GOOD WITH ROASTED CHUNKS OF BUTTERNUT SQUASH OR PUMPKIN.

Preparation: 3 minutes; Cooking: 17 minutes

SERVES FOUR TO SIX

INGREDIENTS

50g/2oz/¼ cup butter or 60ml/4 tbsp olive oil
500g/1¼lb shallots or small onions, peeled with root ends intact
15ml/1 tbsp golden caster (superfine) sugar
30ml/2 tbsp red or white wine, Madeira or port

1 Heat the butter or oil in a large frying pan and add the shallots or onions in a single layer. Cook gently, turning occasionally, for about 5 minutes, until they are lightly browned all over.

2 Sprinkle the sugar over the browned shallots and cook gently, turning the shallots in the juices, until the sugar begins to caramelize.

3 Pour the wine, Madeira or port over the caramelized shallots and increase the heat. Let the mixture bubble for 4–5 minutes.

4 Add 150ml/¼ pint/⅔ cup water and seasoning. Cover and cook for 5 minutes, then remove the lid and cook until the liquid evaporates and the shallots are tender and glazed. Adjust the seasoning before serving.

COOK'S TIP
Leaving the root ends of the shallots intact helps to ensure that they do not separate or unravel during cooking, but remain whole. They also look more presentable served in this way.

Energy 96kcal/399kJ; Protein 1.3g; Carbohydrate 5.4g, of which sugars 5.4g; Fat 7.5g, of which saturates 1.1g; Cholesterol 0mg; Calcium 22mg; Fibre 1.2g; Sodium 9mg

SPICY POTATO AND OLIVE SALAD

DELICIOUS WARM OR CHILLED, THIS NEW POTATO SALAD IS ENLIVENED WITH CUMIN AND CORIANDER, THEN DRESSED IN OLIVE OIL AND A FRUITY VINEGAR. IT TASTES GOOD WITH COLD ROAST PORK OR HAM.

Preparation: 5 minutes; Cooking: 10 minutes

SERVES FOUR

INGREDIENTS

8 large new potatoes
a large pinch of salt
a large pinch of sugar
3 garlic cloves, chopped
15ml/1 tbsp vinegar of your choice,
  such as a fruit variety
a large pinch of ground cumin or
  whole cumin seeds
a pinch of cayenne pepper or hot
  paprika, to taste
30–45ml/2–3 tbsp extra virgin
  olive oil
30–45ml/2–3 tbsp chopped fresh
  coriander (cilantro) leaves
10–15 dry-fleshed black
  Mediterranean olives

1 Chop the new potatoes into chunks. Put them in a pan, pour in water to cover and add the salt and sugar. Bring to the boil, then reduce the heat and boil gently for about 10 minutes, or until the potatoes are just tender. Drain well and leave in a colander to cool.

2 When cool enough to handle, slice the potato chunks and put them in a bowl.

3 Sprinkle the garlic, vinegar, cumin and cayenne or paprika over the salad. Drizzle with olive oil and sprinkle over coriander and olives.

Energy 238kcal/998kJ; Protein 4g; Carbohydrate 32.6g, of which sugars 2.9g; Fat 11.1g, of which saturates 1.7g; Cholesterol 0mg; Calcium 49mg; Fibre 3.2g; Sodium 448mg

MASALA BEANS WITH FENUGREEK

THE SECRET OF THIS SUPER-FAST DISH IS THE SPICE MIXTURE THAT COATS THE VEGETABLES.
COOKING IS KEPT TO THE MINIMUM SO THAT INDIVIDUAL FLAVOURS ARE STILL DETECTABLE.
Preparation: 4–5 minutes; Cooking: 10–12 minutes

SERVES FOUR

INGREDIENTS

1 onion
5ml/1 tsp ground cumin
5ml/1 tsp ground coriander
5ml/1 tsp sesame seeds
5ml/1 tsp chilli powder
2.5ml/½ tsp crushed garlic
1.5ml/¼ tsp ground turmeric
5ml/1 tsp salt
30ml/2 tbsp vegetable oil
1 tomato, quartered
225g/8oz/1½ cups green
   beans, blanched
1 bunch fresh fenugreek leaves,
   stems discarded
60ml/4 tbsp chopped fresh
   coriander (cilantro)
15ml/1 tbsp lemon juice

1 Roughly chop the onion. Mix together the cumin and coriander, sesame seeds, chilli powder, garlic, turmeric and salt.

2 Put the chopped onion and spice mixture into a food processor or blender, and process for 30–45 seconds until you have a rough paste.

3 In a wok or large, heavy pan, heat the oil over a medium heat and fry the spice paste for about 5 minutes, stirring the mixture occasionally.

VARIATION
Instead of fresh fenugreek, substitute 15ml/1 tbsp dried fenugreek, which is available from Indian markets.

4 Add the tomato quarters, blanched green beans, fresh fenugreek and chopped coriander.

5 Stir-fry the contents of the pan for about 5 minutes, then sprinkle in the lemon juice and serve.

Energy 70kcal/289kJ; Protein 1.6g; Carbohydrate 2.7g, of which sugars 2.1g; Fat 6g, of which saturates 0.7g; Cholesterol 0mg; Calcium 47mg; Fibre 2g; Sodium 6mg

DESSERTS

It's so easy to throw a speedy dessert together, but it's amazing how many of us still opt for shop-bought sweet treats, where the sugar fix comes at a considerable price. This dainty selection scores highly on health thanks to its focus on fruit and spices. You'll find some deliciously creative combinations of soft, firm and dried fruits in dessert-style salads, while the use of spirits and fortified wines in tandem with sugar, honey and spices creates some wonderful fruits-in-syrup type offerings. For example, the presence of a simple sweet sauce in the recipe for Grapefruit in Honey and Whisky really softens the sharpness of that fruit, while still producing a dessert that is fresh and full of zing. Similarly, sweet dessert wine, orange liqueur, citrus peel and cinnamon create an indulgent liquid base for soaking clementines. Honey Baked Figs with Hazelnut Ice Cream is pure delight — and the ice cream can be made easily, too. Of course, no collection of desserts should be without an indulgent chocolate pudding. The classic recipe for Chocolate Fudge Sundaes is a fabulous finale to any meal, or can be enjoyed as a super-fast sweet treat on a relaxing night in.

Left: Combining dried and fresh fruits in a salad is rarely thought of, but well worth the experiment: the sweet taste and chewiness of the preserved fruits perfectly balances fresh, juicy berries and crisp firmer fruits. The fruits can be varied according to taste, but don't forget the cinnamon and honey.

GRAPEFRUIT IN HONEY AND WHISKY

CREATE A SIMPLE YET ELEGANT DESSERT BY ARRANGING A COLOURFUL FAN OF PINK, RED AND WHITE
GRAPEFRUIT SEGMENTS IN A SWEET WHISKY SAUCE. THIS DESSERT IS PERFECT AFTER A RICH MEAL.

Preparation: 4 minutes; Cooking: 14 minutes; Chilling recommended

SERVES FOUR

INGREDIENTS
  1 pink grapefruit
  1 red grapefruit
  1 white grapefruit
  50g/2oz/¼ cup sugar
  60ml/4 tbsp clear honey
  45ml/3 tbsp whisky
  mint leaves, to decorate

1 Cut a thin slice of peel and pith from each end of the grapefruit. Place the cut side down on a plate and cut off the peel and pith in strips. Remove any remaining pith. Cut out each segment leaving the membrane behind. Put the segments into a shallow bowl.

2 Put the sugar and 150ml/¼ pint/ ⅔ cup water into a heavy pan. Bring to the boil, stirring constantly, until the sugar has completely dissolved, then simmer, without stirring, for 10 minutes, until thickened and syrupy.

3 Heat the honey in a pan and boil until it becomes a slightly deeper colour and begins to caramelize. Remove the pan from the heat, add the whisky and, using a match or taper, carefully ignite, if you like, then pour the mixture into the sugar syrup.

VARIATION
The whisky can be replaced with brandy, Cointreau or Grand Marnier.

4 Bring to the boil, and pour over the grapefruit segments. Cover and leave until cold. To serve, put the grapefruit segments on to four serving plates, alternating the colours, pour over some of the syrup and decorate with the mint leaves.

Energy 154kcal/649kJ; Protein 1.1g; Carbohydrate 32.7g, of which sugars 32.7g; Fat 0.1g, of which saturates 0g; Cholesterol 0mg; Calcium 35mg; Fibre 1.6g; Sodium 6mg

HONEY BAKED FIGS WITH HAZELNUT ICE CREAM

FIGS BAKED IN A LEMON-GRASS SCENTED HONEY SYRUP HAVE THE MOST WONDERFUL FLAVOUR, ESPECIALLY WHEN SERVED WITH A GOOD-QUALITY ICE CREAM DOTTED WITH ROASTED HAZELNUTS.

Preparation: 4 minutes; Cooking: 16 minutes

SERVES FOUR

INGREDIENTS

1 lemon grass stalk, finely chopped
1 cinnamon stick, roughly broken
60ml/4 tbsp clear honey
200ml/7fl oz/scant 1 cup water
75g/3oz/¾ cup hazelnuts
8 large ripe dessert figs
400ml/14fl oz/1⅔ cups good-quality
    vanilla ice cream
30ml/2 tbsp hazelnut liqueur
    (optional)

1 Preheat the oven to 190°C/375°F/ Gas 5. Make the syrup by mixing the lemon grass, cinnamon stick, honey and measured water in a small pan. Heat gently, stirring until the honey has dissolved, then bring to the boil. Simmer for 2 minutes.

2 Meanwhile spread out the hazelnuts on a baking sheet and grill (broil) under a medium heat until golden brown. Shake the sheet occasionally, so that they are evenly toasted.

3 Cut the figs into quarters, leaving them intact at the bases. Stand in a baking dish, pour the syrup over and cover tightly with foil and bake for 13–15 minutes until the figs are tender.

4 While the figs are baking, remove the ice cream from the freezer and let soften slightly. Chop the hazelnuts roughly and beat the softened ice cream briefly with an electric beater, then beat in the nuts.

5 To serve, puddle a little of the syrup from the figs on to each dessert plate. Arrange the figs on top and add a spoonful of ice cream. Spoon a little hazelnut liqueur over the ice cream if you like.

COOK'S TIP
If the hazelnut skins need to be removed, tip the nuts into a clean dish towel and rub them off.

Energy 433kcal/1816kJ; Protein 7.8g; Carbohydrate 53.6g, of which sugars 52.1g; Fat 21.2g, of which saturates 7g; Cholesterol 24mg; Calcium 227mg; Fibre 4.2g; Sodium 88mg

FRESH FRUIT SALAD

ORANGES ARE AN ESSENTIAL INGREDIENT FOR A SUCCESSFUL AND REFRESHING FRUIT SALAD, WHICH CAN INCLUDE ANY FRUIT IN SEASON. A COLOURFUL COMBINATION TAKES JUST MINUTES TO MAKE.

Preparation: 6 minutes; Cooking: 0 minutes

SERVES SIX

INGREDIENTS
2 apples
2 oranges
2 peaches
16–20 strawberries
30ml/2 tbsp lemon juice
15–30ml/1–2 tbsp orange
   flower water
icing (confectioners') sugar,
   to taste (optional)

COOK'S TIP
The easiest way to remove the pith and peel from an orange is to cut a thin slice from each end of the orange first, using a sharp knife. It will then be easier to cut off the remaining peel and pith.

1 Peel and core the apples and cut into thin slices. Remove the pith and peel from the oranges and cut each one into segments. Squeeze the juice from the membrane and retain.

2 Blanch the peaches for 1 minute in boiling water. Peel and slice thickly.

3 Hull and halve the strawberries, and place all the fruit in a large bowl.

4 Blend together the lemon juice, orange flower water and any reserved orange juice. Taste and add a little icing sugar to sweeten, if you like. Pour the fruit juice over the salad and serve.

Energy 42kcal/180kJ; Protein 1.1g; Carbohydrate 9.8g, of which sugars 9.8g; Fat 0.1g, of which saturates 0g; Cholesterol 0mg; Calcium 28mg; Fibre 1.9g; Sodium 5mg

DRIED FRUIT SALAD

THIS DESSERT DOESN'T TAKE LONG TO PREPARE, BUT MUST BE MADE AHEAD OF TIME, TO ALLOW THE DRIED FRUIT TO PLUMP UP AND FLAVOURS TO BLEND. IT IS ALSO GOOD FOR BREAKFAST.

Preparation: 6 minutes; Cooking: 12 minutes; Make ahead

SERVES FOUR

INGREDIENTS
115g/4oz/½ cup ready-to-eat dried
   apricots, halved
115g/4oz/½ cup ready-to-eat dried
   peaches, halved
1 pear
1 apple
1 orange
115g/4oz/1 cup mixed raspberries
   and blackberries
1 cinnamon stick
50g/2oz/¼ cup caster
   (superfine) sugar
15ml/1 tbsp clear honey
30ml/2 tbsp lemon juice

1 Place the dried fruit in a large pan and add 600ml/1 pint/2½ cups water.

2 Peel and core the pear and apple, then dice. Remove peel and pith from the orange and cut into wedges. Add all the cut fruit to the pan with the raspberries and blackberries.

3 Pour in a further 150ml/¼ pint/⅔ cup water, the cinnamon, sugar and honey, and bring to the boil. Cover and simmer for 10 minutes, then remove the pan from the heat. Stir in the lemon juice. Leave to cool completely, then transfer the fruit and syrup to a bowl and chill for 1–2 hours before serving.

Energy 190kcal/811kJ; Protein 3.3g; Carbohydrate 46g, of which sugars 46g; Fat 0.5g, of which saturates 0g; Cholesterol 0mg; Calcium 75mg; Fibre 6g; Sodium 13mg

CHOCOLATE FUDGE SUNDAES

YOU COULD PUT ON WEIGHT JUST READING THE INGREDIENTS LIST, BUT WHAT A LOVELY WAY TO DO IT. ICE CREAM, BANANAS, ALMONDS AND RICH MOCHA SYRUP MAKE FOR SHEER INDULGENCE.

Preparation: 10 minutes; Cooking: 6 minutes

SERVES FOUR

INGREDIENTS

    4 scoops each vanilla and coffee
      ice cream
    2 small ripe bananas, sliced
    whipped cream
    toasted flaked (sliced) almonds
For the sauce
    50g/2oz/¼ cup soft light brown sugar
    120ml/4fl/oz/½ cup golden (light
      corn) syrup
    45ml/3 tbsp strong black coffee
    5ml/1 tsp ground cinnamon
    150g/5oz plain (semisweet)
      chocolate, chopped
    75ml/3fl oz/⅓ cup whipping cream
    45ml/3 tbsp coffee liqueur (optional)

1 To make the sauce, place the sugar, syrup, coffee and cinnamon in a heavy pan. Simmer for around 5 minutes, stirring constantly with a spoon.

2 Turn off the heat and stir in the chocolate. When melted and smooth, stir in the cream and liqueur.

3 Fill four glasses with one scoop of vanilla and another of coffee ice cream.

4 Arrange the sliced bananas over the ice cream. Pour the warm fudge sauce over the bananas, then top each sundae with a generous swirl of whipped cream. Sprinkle toasted almonds over the cream and serve at once.

VARIATION

This is a great dessert for special occasions, and you can ring the changes through the year by choosing other flavours of ice cream such as strawberry, toffee or chocolate. In the summer, substitute raspberries or strawberries for the bananas, and sprinkle chopped roasted hazelnuts on top in place of the flaked (sliced) almonds.

Energy 595kcal/2498kJ; Protein 6.3g; Carbohydrate 88.1g, of which sugars 85.3g; Fat 26.5g, of which saturates 14.1g; Cholesterol 26mg; Calcium 139mg; Fibre 1.8g; Sodium 144mg

CLEMENTINES WITH STAR ANISE

LOOKING DRAMATIC, WITH THE DARK STARS OF ANISE AGAINST THE SUNSHINE ORANGE CLEMENTINES, THIS IS A SIMPLY DELICIOUS DESSERT. IT TASTES BEST CHILLED, SO ALLOW TIME FOR THAT.
Preparation: 6–8 minutes; Cooking: 12 minutes; Chilling recommended

SERVES SIX

INGREDIENTS
  1 lime
  350ml/12fl oz/1½ cups sweet
    dessert wine, such as Sauternes
  75g/3oz/6 tbsp caster
    (superfine) sugar
  6 star anise
  1 cinnamon stick
  1 vanilla pod (bean)
  30ml/2 tbsp Cointreau or other
    orange liqueur
  12 clementines

VARIATION
Tangerines or seedless oranges can be
used instead of clementines.

1 Thinly pare 1 or 2 strips of rind from
the lime. Put them in a pan, with the
wine, sugar, star anise and cinnamon.
Split the vanilla pod and add it to the
pan. Bring to the boil, then lower the
heat and simmer for 10 minutes.

2 Remove the pan from the heat and
leave to cool, then stir in the liqueur.

3 Peel the clementines. Cut some of
them in half and place them all in a
dish. Pour over the wine and chill.

Energy 149kcal/632kJ; Protein 0.9g; Carbohydrate 24.7g, of which sugars 24.7g; Fat 0.1g, of which saturates 0g; Cholesterol 0mg; Calcium 40mg; Fibre 1g; Sodium 12mg

INDEX